ASSEMBLIES FOR THE PRIMARIES

Compiled by

A. G. PATSTON

Author of the *Visual Bible*
and *Visual Story of Christianity* series

THE RELIGIOUS EDUCATION PRESS LTD.

HEADINGTON HILL HALL   OXFORD

PERGAMON PRESS LTD.

OXFORD · LONDON · EDINBURGH

NEW YORK · TORONTO · SYDNEY

Copyright © 1969 A. G. PATSTON

First Edition 1969

Library of Congress Catalog Card No. 72–80292

Printed in Great Britain by A. Wheaton & Co., Exeter

08 006440 X

ASSEMBLIES FOR THE PRIMARIES

CONTENTS

AUTUMN

v

DECEMBER

SPRING

JANUARY

FEBRUARY

MARCH

APRIL

SUMMER

MAY

JUNE

JULY

INTRODUCTION

'The Act of Worship provides an occasion when the school meets together as a community to bring before God the concern of the school and of the world outside.' (*School Worship*, ILEA). This book contains daily services for the primary school throughout the year and includes the festivals and special days in due season. A theme is provided—and the hymns and prayers, stories and readings, carry this theme through each act of worship. A familiar framework for the order of service is maintained to avoid confusion and to keep a serene atmosphere.

STORIES

These form an important part of the services. They are intended to seize the interest of the young children and are written to be 'read aloud'.

PRAYERS

'Prayer is conversation with God' and the language used is relevant to the age-group. The more difficult traditional prayers of the Church are included to introduce gradually our national heritage.

The Lord's Prayer

The daily use of this prayer could be optional as too frequent repetition may lead to indifference.

HYMNS

The hymns selected have been taken from three hymn books, all published by the Oxford University Press:

> DS *The Daily Service.*
> SP *Songs of Praise.*
> IP *Infant Praise.*

The hymns are chosen for the younger child, but no suitable hymn has been rejected because of difficult words. Infants usually learn their hymns by heart, but hymn books should be available for the juniors.

1

Music makes an important contribution to the worship of God and the children should enter and leave the hall or room while music is played, either live or recorded.

POEMS AND READINGS

These are included to allow individual children to play a part in the conduct of morning assembly. The Bible is a difficult book for the younger child to read and, for this reason, the extracts have usually been taken from the *New English Bible* and kept to the minimum. They are reproduced by permission*.

ORGANISATION

Consideration has been given to the limited space that is available in halls and to the problem of children being crowded together. The order of the services allows for alternate standing and sitting, but unnecessary movement has been kept to the minimum.   A. G. P.

AUTUMN   1   SEPTEMBER

THE NEW TERM

Beginning of Term

O come, let us worship and bow down, let us kneel before the Lord our Maker. For He is our God.

THEME:
As we stand before the new term, let us thank God for all new beginnings and the chance to begin again where we have failed.

PRAYER:
O Lord, our Heavenly Father, Creator of the wonderful world, who in the beginning did make everything good, be near to us as we begin our new term at school. Help us to find joy in a fresh beginning and to do all our work with an eager and willing spirit, that we may be fit and useful followers of Jesus all our lives. *Amen.*

HYMN: Lord, behold us with Thy blessing (*DS* 163; *SP* 333).
or
Holy, holy, holy! Lord God Almighty (*DS* 4; *SP* 187).

PRAYER:
We thank Thee, Heavenly Father, for all the blessings that you have given us. For the joy of our holidays and for the strength we have gained from them. Bless, we beseech Thee, this our school, and may we go forward together in wisdom and knowledge and in favour with Thee. Through Jesus Christ our Lord. *Amen.*

CHORAL SPEAKING:
The School Creed
This is our school,
Let peace dwell here,
Let the room be full of contentment,
Let love abide here,

3

Love of one another,
Love of mankind,
Love of life itself,
And love of God.
Let us remember
That, as many hands build a house,
So many hearts make a school.

STORY LESSON: *In the Steps of the Master* (page 147).

UNISON PRAYER:

The Prayer of Dedication

Jesus, Friend of the friendless;
Helper of the poor; Healer of the sick;
Whose life was spent in doing good; Let us follow in Thy footsteps.
Make us strong to do right; Gentle with the weak; And kind to
all who are in sorrow;
That we may be like Thee, our Lord and Master. *Amen.*

THE LORD'S PRAYER.

HYMN: O Jesus, I have promised (*DS* 39; *SP* 255).
or
God whose name is Love (*SP* 359).

CLOSING:

May the blessing of God Almighty, the Father, the Son, and the
Holy Spirit, rest upon us and upon all our work and worship done
in His Name. May He give us light to guide us, courage to support
us, and love to unite us, now and for evermore. *Amen.*

AUTUMN 2 SEPTEMBER

CONTENTMENT

OPENING:

This is the day which the Lord hath made. We will rejoice and be
glad in it. (Psa. *118*. 24).

THEME:
   Jesus said to His disciples: 'Therefore, I bid you put away anxious thoughts about food to keep you alive and clothes to cover your body. Life is more than food, the body more than clothes.'

HYMN: Glad that I live am I (*DS* 114; *SP* 499).

UNISON PRAYER:

> Be Thou with us every day,
> In our work and in our play,
> When we learn and when we pray.
> Hear us, Holy Jesus.
>
> Make us brave, without a fear,
> Make us happy, full of cheer,
> Sure that Thou art always near.
> Hear us, Holy Jesus.
>
> May we grow from day to day,
> Glad to learn each holy way,
> Ever ready to obey.
> Hear us, Holy Jesus. *Amen.*

BIBLE READING: The lilies of the field (Luke *12.* 22–31 *NEB*).

STORY LESSON: *The Man who Sold his Shadow* (page 147).

PRAYER:
   O Loving Father, thank you for taking care of us through the night. Help us today to do our best at work and at play.
   Help us to do our work well, even though it may be difficult, and to find the sunshine even among the shadows. *Amen.*

HYMN: Lord of all hopefulness, Lord of all joy (*DS* 79; *SP* 565).
   or
   He who would valiant be (*DS* 74; *SP* 515).

THE LORD'S PRAYER.

SILENT PRAYER:
   A moment of silence to thank God for His gifts to each one of us.

5

Unto God, who is able to supply all our needs, be all glory and honour for ever and ever. *Amen.*

AUTUMN 3 SEPTEMBER

COURAGE

Grace Darling, 7 September 1838

OPENING:

They that wait upon the Lord shall renew their strength; they shall mount up with wings as eagles; they shall run and not be weary; they shall walk and not faint. (Isa. *40.* 31).

THEME:

Let us ask God for courage in times of difficulty or danger.

PRAYER:

The Prayer for Protection

O God, Thou hast made us, and Thou wilt keep us. We are never alone, for Thou art always by our side and we are safe with Thee. Help us to fear nothing; to be brave, and always to trust Thee, through Jesus Christ our Lord. *Amen. (Daily Service,* OUP).

HYMN: Fight the good fight with all thy might (*DS* 69; *SP* 491)
　　　　or
　　　　Father, hear the prayer we offer (*DS* 123; *SP* 487).

CHORAL SPEAKING: I will lift up mine eyes unto the hills (Psa. *121*).

STORY LESSON: *The Day of the Rescue* (page 148).

PRAYER:

Almighty God, we thank Thee for all brave people who offer their lives to help others. Give them courage and cheerfulness as they help those in need and strengthen us with a desire to follow their great example. Through Jesus Christ our Lord. *Amen.*

HYMN: The Lord's my Shepherd (*DS* 214).

PRAYER:

Jesus said, 'Let not your heart be troubled, neither let it be afraid.'

THE LORD'S PRAYER.

CLOSING:

May the grace of courage, gaiety, and the quiet mind, with all such blessedness as belongs to the Father in Heaven be ours; to the praise of the Father, Son, and Holy Spirit, Who ever liveth and reigneth, one God, world without end. *Amen.*

AUTUMN   4   SEPTEMBER

THE CHURCH

Holy Cross Day, 14 September

OPENING:

God is a Spirit, and they that worship Him, must worship Him in spirit and in truth.

THEME:

The Church remembers this special day when the first Christian Emperor, Constantine the Great, built two churches. One on Calvary, where Jesus was crucified, and one on the place of the tomb, where Jesus rose from the dead. Let us remember the work of the Church.

PRAYER:

O God our Father, we thank you for the Church throughout the world. Help us to remember it is your house and may we now, together, lift up our hearts and voices in praise and thanks to you. *Amen.*

HYMN: All people that on earth do dwell (*DS* 1; *SP* 443).

BIBLE READING: Who do men say that the Son of Man is? (Mat. *16*. 13–20 *NEB*).

STORY LESSON: *The Church in a House* (page 149).

PRAYER:

A Litany for the Church

For cathedrals and churches in cities and countries everywhere,
  (*Together*) *We thank Thee, Heavenly Father.*
For builders, artists, and craftsmen who have laboured to build to Thy honour and glory,
  We thank Thee, Heavenly Father.
For boys and girls of all nations who join together in worshipping Thee,
  We thank Thee, Heavenly Father.
For all who belong to Thy Church and are met together in Thy Name,
  We thank Thee, Heavenly Father. Amen.

THE LORD'S PRAYER.

HYMN: Praise, my soul, the King of heaven (*DS* 25; *SP* 623).

CLOSING:

Now unto Him who is able to do exceeding abundantly above all that we ask or think according to the power that worketh in us, unto Him be glory in the Church and in Christ Jesus throughout all ages, world without end. *Amen.*

AUTUMN   5   SEPTEMBER

ST. MATTHEW

St. Matthew's Day, 21 September

OPENING:

Jesus said, 'If you dwell in me, and my words dwell in you, ask what you will, and you shall have it. This is my Father's glory,

8

that you may bear fruit in plenty and so be my disciples.' (John *15.*
7 *NEB*).

THEME:

In September is the special day for St. Matthew, one of the disciples of Jesus. Here is a poem about the disciples.

POETRY READING: *Come, follow Me!* (page 131).

PRAYER:

Lord Jesus, who didst call a company of friends together to spread the Gospel in all the world, help us to follow Thee like the disciples of old. Help us, like Matthew, to see the right path and to follow Thee in the way of truth and service for others. We ask this in Thy Name. *Amen.*

HYMN: Onward, Christian soldiers! (*DS* 139; *SP* 397).

STORY LESSON: *The Calling of St. Matthew* (page 150).

BIBLE READING:

Matthew was once a rich tax-collector. These words are from his book in the Bible.
Do not store up for yourselves treasure on earth (Mat. *6.* 19–21 *NEB*).

PRAYER:

The Prayer for Goodwill

O Lord and Saviour, who by Thy words and Thy Life has taught us how true men should live, grant unto us now and at all times Thy spirit of kindliness and goodwill. Inspire in our hearts Thy love for God and men and help us all our days to follow humbly in Thy footsteps. *Amen.*

UNISON PRAYER:

Lord of the loving heart, may mine be loving too.
Lord of the gentle hands, may mine be gentle too.
Lord of the willing feet, may mine be willing too.
So may I grow, more like to Thee,
In all I say and do. *Amen.*

9

CLOSING:

The Prayer for Friends

Receive into Thy sure keeping, O God, ourselves and all those we
love, and teach us to put our trust in Thee. Through Jesus Christ
our Lord. *Amen.*

AUTUMN 6 SEPTEMBER

HARVEST FESTIVAL

Autumn Days

OPENING:

Make a joyful song unto God, all the earth.
Sing forth the glory of His name.
All the earth shall worship Thee,
They shall sing to Thy Name.
O bless our God, ye peoples
And make the voice of His praise to be heard.

THEME:

Let us praise God for His harvest gifts.

HYMN: Come, ye thankful people, come (*DS* 109; *SP* 9).

PRAYER:

O Lord, our Heavenly Father, we thank Thee for Thy gifts at
harvest time. For the corn and fruit of the field and orchard, for
the harvest of the sea and for all useful things from the mines
beneath the earth. May we, who have plenty, remember those in
need and may we never waste Thy gifts but use them and share
them for the sake of Him who lived and died for us, Jesus Christ
our Lord. *Amen.*

BIBLE READING:

And God said, Let the waters under the heaven be gathered together unto one place, and let the dry land appear; and it was so. And God called the dry land Earth; and the gathering together of the waters called he Seas; and God saw that it was good. (Gen. *1.* 9–10).

HYMN: All things bright and beautiful (*DS* 17; *SP* 444).

POETRY READING: *Out in the Fields with God* (page 131).

STORY LESSON: *The Gift of the Rice Harvest* (page 151).

PRAYER:

A Litany of Harvest Thanksgiving
For fields of corn and golden wheat,
For oats and barley, bread to eat,
For orchards ripe, when Autumn comes
With apples, pears, and purple plums,
    (*Together*) *We thank Thee, Heavenly Father.*

For shoals of fish from oceans deep,
For men who labour while we sleep,
For mines deep down beneath the ground,
Where oil and coal and iron are found,
    We thank Thee, Heavenly Father.

For shining sun and gentle rain
That brings the harvest time again,
For all Thy gifts, to Thee we bring
Our Harvest time thankoffering.   . .
    We thank Thee, Heavenly Father.

SILENT PRAYER:
A moment of silent prayer for God's gifts to each one of us.

THE LORD'S PRAYER.

HYMN: We plough the fields and scatter (*DS* 111; *SP* 14).

CLOSING:
While the earth remaineth
Seedtime and harvest

And cold and heat
And summer and winter, and day and night, shall not cease.
To Him, from whom cometh every good and perfect gift be all
honour and glory, world without end. *Amen.*

AUTUMN   7   SEPTEMBER

AUTUMN LEAVES

Autumn Days

OPENING:

To God, our Father, now we bring
Our prayers and hymns of praise.
To God, who gives us everything,
Our thanks for Autumn days.

He sends the sun to swell the grain,
He sends the wind among the trees,
And when the earth is bare again
He covers it with golden leaves.

THEME:

Today we are going to think about falling leaves, and praise God
for the beauty of their autumn colouring.

PRAYER:

For falling leaves, all brown and yellow-gold,
And pink, and glowing red like fiery flames,
For lovely rustling sounds the drifted heaps
Make, as we run among them at our games.
For all the work you do to make the world
A pleasant place of colour, scent and sound.
We bring our thanks, O God, this autumn day
And praise you for the glories all around. *Amen.*

HYMN: For the beauty of the earth (*DS* 113; *SP* 494).

STORY LESSON: *The Friendly Trees* (page 152).

POETRY READING: *Autumn Leaves* (page 132).

PRAYER:

We praise Thee, O God, for all the sights and sounds of the changing seasons and for the joys of Autumn days. Thank you for the green of the leaves turning to red and gold and falling down to feed the earth that we may have new leaves in the coming year. For these Thy gifts to us, we thank Thee. *Amen.*

THE LORD'S PRAYER.

HYMN: All things which live below the sky (*DS* 18; *SP* 445).

CLOSING:

From the rising of the sun unto the going down of the same the Lord's name be praised. *Amen.*

AUTUMN   8   SEPTEMBER

ST. JEROME

St. Jerome's Day, 30 September

OPENING:

Let us praise God for all good people of long ago who placed their trust in the Lord.

THEME:

In September is the special day for St. Jerome, who lived and worked that we might know more about the Bible.

PRAYER:

O Lord, our Heavenly Father, we thank you for the saints who lived long ago and who have worked for you on earth. We thank you for the work of St. Jerome, who taught us more about the

13

Bible, and we pray this morning that we, too, can follow his example of love and kindness. For Jesus Christ's sake. *Amen.*

HYMN: For all the saints (*DS* 97; *SP* 202)
or
Holy, holy, holy! Lord God Almighty (*DS* 4; *SP* 187).

UNISON PRAYER:

Lord of the loving heart, may mine be loving too.
Lord of the gentle hands, may mine be gentle too.
Lord of the willing feet, may mine be willing too.
So may I grow, more like to Thee,
In all I say and do. *Amen.*

STORY LESSON: *St. Jerome and the Lion* (page 153).

UNISON PRAYER:

A Child's Prayer
Father, we thank Thee for the night
And for the pleasant morning light;
For rest and food and loving care
And all that makes the day so fair.
Help us to do the things we should,
To be to others kind and good.
In all we do, in all we say,
To follow Jesus every day. *Amen.*

SILENT PRAYER:
Let us think how we can work for Jesus every day.

THE LORD'S PRAYER.

HYMN: Little drops of water (*DS* 78; *SP* 365)
or
Father, we thank thee for the night (*DS* 146; *SP* 355).

CLOSING:
Grant us, O Lord, the spirit to think and do always such things as are right; that we, who cannot do anything that is good without Thee, may be enabled to live according to Thy Will. Through Jesus Christ our Lord. *Amen.*

14

HOMES AND FAMILIES

OPENING:

Jesus said, 'In my Father's house are many mansions; if it were not so, I would have told you. I go to prepare a place for you. And if I go and prepare a place for you, I will come again, and receive you unto myself; that where I am, there ye may be also.' (John *14. 2 AV*.)

THEME:

Today we are going to think of our homes and to thank God for them.

PRAYER:

As the sparrow builds her house and the swallow her nest, we thank you Father God that we, too, have homes and are surrounded by Thy love and care, day by day. Help us to share gladly and to be kind to one another so that our homes may be full of joy, for Jesus Christ's sake. *Amen.*

HYMN: Through the night thy angels kept (*SP* 375)
 or
The Holy Child went to and fro (*IP* 68).

BIBLE READING:

Jesus loved going to people's homes. One day, he went to the home of a friend where there was a little boy. Let us listen to what happened there.
(The disciples argue (Mark *9.* 33–37 *NEB*).)

STORY LESSON: *The House with the Golden Windows* (page 154).

UNISON PRAYER:

Dear Heavenly Father,
Thank you for taking care of us through the night.
Help us to please you all day long.
May we learn to help one another
And those at home.

Bless our fathers and mothers
And all children all over the world.
For Thy sake. *Amen.*

SILENT PRAYER:

Let us, in silence, say 'thank you' to God for our homes and parents.

THE LORD'S PRAYER.

Jesus often stayed at another home in Bethany; the home of two sisters named Martha and Mary. While Martha bustled about getting the meal ready, Mary loved to listen to the words of Jesus.

BIBLE READING:

Martha and Mary at Bethany (Luke *10.* 38–42 *NEB*).

HYMN: Jesus, good above all other (*DS* 125; *SP* 540).

CLOSING:

The grace of our Lord Jesus Christ, and the love of God, and the fellowship of the Holy Spirit, be with us all, now and for evermore. *Amen.*

AUTUMN   10   OCTOBER

KINDNESS TO ANIMALS

St. Francis's Day, 4 October

OPENING:

All things which live below the sky,
Or move within the sea,
Are creatures of the Lord most high,
And brothers unto me.

THEME:

Today we think of St. Francis, who loved all God's family of birds and animals. Let us praise God for all His creatures.

16

PRAYER:

We praise you, Heavenly Father, for the animals who are Thy creatures. We thank you for our pets, at home and at school. May we never be unkind to them, but always to treat them with gentle hands and kindly words. For the sake of Him who loved all helpless things, Jesus Christ our Lord. *Amen.*

HYMN: All things which live below the sky (*DS* 18; *SP* 445).

POETRY READING:

Kindness to Animals (page 132)

HYMN: God of the rabbits, keep them warm, (*IP* 5).

STORY LESSON: *Brother Francis and the Wolf* (page 155).

PRAYER:

A Prayer of St. Francis

Praised be my Lord, for our Brother Sun,
Thou caused all day his course to run.
For our Sister Moon, praised be the Lord
By stars in heavenly hosts adored.
For our Brothers, the Wind, the Cloud, and the Air
Whose blessings all Thy creatures share.
Praised be my Lord for Waters bright,
For our Brother Fire, his warmth and light,
To Mother Earth, Thy gifts you send,
O God our Father and our Friend. *Amen.*

SILENT PRAYER:

Let us think how we can take greater care of our pets.

THE LORD'S PRAYER.

HYMN: I love God's tiny creatures (*DS* 22; *SP* 361).

CLOSING:

Almighty Father, King of Kings,
The lover of the meek,
Make me a friend of helpless things,
Defender of the weak. *Amen.*

17

ADVENTURE AND DISCOVERY
Columbus Day, 12 October

OPENING:

The earth is the Lord's and the fulness thereof; the world and they that dwell therein. In His hands are the deep places of the earth, and the strength of the hills is His also.

THEME:

In the month of October 1492 Columbus discovered the New World of America. Let us praise God for all brave people who venture into the unknown.

PRAYER:

O Lord, our Heavenly Father, keep alive in our hearts the spirit of adventure which makes men scorn the way of safety so that Thy will be done. Help us to be worthy of those brave people who in every age have ventured all in obedience to Thy call; through Jesus Christ our Lord. *Amen.*

HYMN: He who would valiant be (*DS* 74; *SP* 515).

UNISON PRAYER:

The Prayer of St. Ignatius of Loyola

Teach us, good Lord, to serve Thee as Thou deservest.
To give and not to count the cost.
To fight and not to heed the wounds.
To toil and not to seek for rest.
To labour and not to ask for any reward
Save that of knowing that we do Thy will. *Amen.*

STORY LESSON: *Columbus Finds the New World* (page 155).

PRAYER:

Here is the prayer of Sir Francis Drake, another great explorer.

O Lord God, when Thou givest to Thy servants to endeavour any great matter, grant us also to know that it is not the beginning but the continuing of the same unto the end, until it be thoroughly finished, which yields the true glory. Through Him who for the finishing of Thy work laid down His life—Jesus Christ our Lord. *Amen.*

THE LORD'S PRAYER.

HYMN: Jesus shall reign where'er the sun (*DS* 138; *SP* 545)
or
Far round the world (*DS* 135; *SP* 299).

CLOSING:

Go forth into the world in peace; be of good courage; hold fast that which is good; strengthen the faint-hearted and support the weak; love and serve the Lord, rejoicing in the power of the Holy Spirit.

And the blessing of God Almighty, the Father, the Son and the Holy Spirit, be upon you and remain with you always. *Amen.*

AUTUMN   12   OCTOBER

ST. LUKE

St. Luke's Day, 18 October

OPENING:

Love the Lord your God with all your heart, with all your soul, with all your strength, and with all your mind; and your neighbour as yourself.

THEME:

In October is the special day for St. Luke, who wrote the third book in the New Testament. He was a doctor, and only in his book do we read how Jesus healed the ten lepers.

BIBLE READING: The healing of the ten lepers
(Luke *17*. 11–19 *NEB*).

HYMN: Thine arm, O Lord, in days of old (*DS* 159; *SP* 287).

PRAYER:

In the Bible story Jesus healed ten lepers—but only one came back to say 'thank you'. Let us not forget to thank God for His care.

> God and Father of us all,
> Hear us, as we bow in prayer.
> Fill our hearts with love to Thee
> As we thank Thee for Thy care.
>
> Us, Thy children, Thou hast kept
> Safe from dangers, great and small;
> Thou dost guard us, day and night,
> God and Father of us all. *Amen.*

STORY LESSON:

It is only in the book of St. Luke that we find the beautiful story of the Good Samaritan. Let us hear how it happened.
The Good Samaritan (page 156).

PRAYER:

Almighty God, who didst call Luke the Doctor to be a follower and to write down the Good News of Jesus, may we learn the great lesson of the Good Samaritan. Help us to be kind to others at all times and to remember that our neighbours are those who need our help and friendship, wherever they may be. *Amen.*

SILENT PRAYER:

Let us think of somebody who may be needing our help at this time.

THE LORD'S PRAYER.

HYMN: Father, we thank Thee for the night (*DS* 146; *SP* 355).

CLOSING:

> May the grace of Christ uphold us
> And the Father's love enfold us;
> May the Holy Spirit guide us
> And all joy and peace betide us;
> Now and through eternity. *Amen.*

TRUSTWORTHINESS

OPENING:

Heavenly Father, we draw near Thee
With the voice of joy and praise;
Bless us as we stand before Thee,
Teach us more about Thy ways.
May we praise Thee, may we praise Thee,
Love and serve Thee all our days.

HYMN: Soldiers of Christ arise (*DS* 85; *SP* 641).

THEME:

Can you be trusted to work on your own? Can you be trusted to
do what is right when no one is watching over you? This story
from the Bible is about a man who trusted his servants when he
went away on a long journey.

BIBLE READING: The ten talents (Mat. *25*. 14–29 *NEB*).

PRAYER:

Lord Jesus, who at Gethsemane didst stand alone in all the world,
give us courage to be trustworthy in all that we do. Strengthen our
characters so that our word may be trusted by all whom we meet.
Help us to do our duty without hope of reward and to do our work
thoroughly, whether it be for ourselves or others. We ask it for
Thy Name's sake. *Amen.*

HYMN: O Jesus, I have promised (*DS* 39; *SP* 255).

STORY LESSON: *Hans the Shepherd Boy* (page 157).

PRAYER:

O Lord, our Heavenly Father, give us always courage to be true
and to do what we know is right, even if it means standing alone.
Help us to be trustworthy in all our work and faithful in the little
things, so that when we grow up we may be trusted in the big
things of life. Help us to become fellow workers with Thy Son,
Jesus Christ our Lord. *Amen.*

THE LORD'S PRAYER.

HYMN: Stand up, stand up, for Jesus (*DS* 141; *SP* 646).

CLOSING:

> Help us to be kind and true,
> Thy good work on earth to do.
> All we have with others share
> Every day and everywhere. *Amen.*

AUTUMN   14   OCTOBER

HARVEST OF THE SEA

Fisherman's Moon

OPENING:

> They that go down to the sea in ships, that do business in great
> waters; these see the works of the Lord, and his wonders in the
> deep. (Psa. *107*. 23–24).

THEME:

> Our thoughts for today are for sailors and fishermen. October is
> the month of the Fishermen's Moon, when the strong tides bring
> great shoals of fish to our shores. Some fishermen say that the
> silvery light of the moon attracts the fish to the surface.

HYMN: When lamps are lighted in the town (*DS* 158; *SP* 378).

PRAYER:

> O Father God, who has made the sea and all that lives therein.
> give Thy blessing on the harvest of the waters that there may be
> plenty; and on the fishermen and sailors that they may be safe
> in every part of the deep. Grant this, O Heavenly Father, for
> Jesus' sake. *Amen.*

BIBLE READING: Peter's great catch of fish (Luke *5*. 1–11 *NEB*).

STORY LESSON: *The Storm on the Sea of Galilee* (page 158).

PRAYER:

We pray to Thee, O God our Heavenly Father, for all those who go down to the sea in ships and work upon the great waters. We ask you to protect all sailors and fishermen, the keepers of the lightships and lighthouses, the pilots of the ports, and those who man our lifeboats and guard our coasts. Keep them free from danger and bring them safely to the haven where they would be, through Jesus Christ, our Lord. *Amen.*

SILENT PRAYER:

Let us think, in silence, of the prayer of the Breton fishermen: 'Dear God, be good to me. The sea is so wide and my boat is so small.'

THE LORD'S PRAYER.

HYMN: Fierce raged the tempest o'er the deep (*DS* 124; *SP* 489).

CLOSING:

The Lord preserve our going out, and our coming in from this time forth, and even for evermore. *Amen.*

AUTUMN   15   OCTOBER

THE WORLD FAMILY
United Nations Day, 24 October

OPENING:

North and south and east and west,
May Thy holy name be blest.
Everywhere beneath the sun
As in heaven, Thy will be done.

23

Today is United Nations Day, when we all remember those who work for the peace of the world and pray for their success. Let us join them in prayer for peace throughout the world.

PRAYER:

Almighty God, Father of all mankind, we think today of children all over the world. May we always remember that people from every land belong to one big family of brothers and sisters. Help us to live together in peace and goodwill, so that Thy kingdom of love and brotherhood may be set up throughout the world. Through Jesus Christ our Lord. *Amen.*

HYMN: Remember all the people (*DS* 140; *SP* 369).

STORY LESSON: *Christ of the Andes* (page 159).

PRAYER:

Heavenly Father, we pray today for all nations of the world. For people of every race and colour, for the millions in the lands and great continents of the world.
(Together) Hear us, Heavenly Father.
May all nations meet together in Thy Name, O Lord, forgetting the quarrels of long ago and their fears, today, of one another.
Hear us, Heavenly Father.
Bless all children everywhere who are hungry and poor, or who have no clothing or homes of their own.
Hear us, Heavenly Father.
We ask Thee to help all those who are working together for the peace of the world. Be with them in their meetings and help them in their difficulties.
Hear us, Heavenly Father. Amen.

THE LORD'S PRAYER.

HYMN: Far round the world (*DS* 135; *SP* 299).

CLOSING:

God be merciful unto us and bless us; and cause His face to shine upon us; that Thy way may be known upon earth, Thy saving health among all nations. *Amen.*

BOOKS AND READING
Alfred the Great, 28 October

THEME:
Let us thank God today for the gift of books and the joy of reading. Let us listen to the reading of a poem.

POETRY READING: *Story Books* (page 133).

HYMN: In our work and in our play (*DS* 77; *SP* 538).

READING:
The second reading is from the Bible:
Happy is the man that findeth wisdom,
And the man that getteth understanding.
For the merchandise of it is better than the merchandise of silver,
And the gain thereof than fine gold.
She is more precious than rubies:
And all the things thou canst desire are not to be compared unto her.
Length of days is in her right hand;
And in her left hand riches and honour.
Her ways are ways of pleasantness,
And all her paths are peace. (Proverbs 3. 13–17).

HYMN: God has given us a book full of stories (*IP* 20).

STORY LESSON: *A Prince Learns to Read* (page 160).

PRAYER:
Heavenly Father, who givest us all things richly to enjoy, we thank you for the gift of books and the joy of reading. We thank you for clever writers who wrote down wonderful stories for us to read, and for the invention of printing. Help all who are learning to read so that they, too, may enjoy the gift that opens wide the door. *Amen.*

THE LORD'S PRAYER.

CLOSING:

Write Thy words of truth in our hearts, O Lord, and help us to treasure Thy message of love and kindness, for ever and ever. *Amen.*

AUTUMN 17 NOVEMBER

SKILL OF OUR HANDS

Sistine Chapel, 1 November

OPENING:

Whatsoever thy hand findeth to do, do it with thy might. (Eccles. *9. 10.).*

THEME:

Let us praise God for the skill of our hands; for painting and drawing, writing and modelling, and all things that our hands can do.

PRAYER:

O God, who has commanded that no one should be idle, give us grace to use all our skills and talents in Thy service and for the service of others; that whatsoever our hands find to do, we may do it with all our might. *Amen.*

HYMN: Lord of health, thou life within us (*DS* 80; *SP* 567).

BIBLE READING: Jesus restores a withered arm (Luke *6.* 6–10 *NEB).*

PRAYER:

A Litany for Clever Hands

For the strength and skill of our hands,
(*Together*) *We give Thee thanks, O Lord.*
For the joy of painting and the beauty of line and colour,
We give Thee thanks, O Lord.

26

For strong and steady fingers to use for model making,
weaving and writing,
We give Thee thanks, O Lord.
For the joy that comes from doing a good piece of work,
even if we have to try and try again,
We give Thee thanks, O Lord.
We praise Thee that Jesus was a carpenter and worked with
His hands. Help us to follow in the way of the Master
Craftsman. *Amen.*

HYMN: Jesus' hands were kind hands, doing good to all (*IP* 70).

STORY LESSON: *Michelangelo* (page 162).

THE LORD'S PRAYER.

HYMN: God who made the earth (*DS* 21; *SP* 358).

CLOSING:
The glorious majesty of the Lord our God be upon us; prosper
Thou the work of our hands upon us, O prosper Thou our handi-
work. *Amen.*

AUTUMN 18 NOVEMBER

FAIR PLAY

OPENING:
Jesus said, 'Do to others as you would have them do to you.'

THEME:
Today we are going to think of being fair and generous to others.
'Happy are the merciful, for it is they who will have mercy shown
to them.'

Help us, O Lord, to be fair in all that we think or speak or do. Make us kindly in thought and generous in deed and to stand for the right against the wrong. Teach us to work as hard and play as fair in Thy sight alone as if all the world saw. Through Jesus Christ our Lord. *Amen.*

BIBLE READING: The labourers in the vineyard (Mat. *20.* 1–16).

HYMN: Heavenly Father may Thy blessing (*DS* 71; *SP* 516).

STORY LESSON: *The Bell in the Market Place* (page 163).

UNISON PRAYER:

Day by day, dear Lord of Thee,
Three things we pray:
    To see Thee more clearly;
    To love Thee more dearly;
    To follow Thee more nearly;
        Day by day. *Amen.*
                (St. Richard of Chichester).

SILENT PRAYER:

O God, give us eyes to see the unhappiness of others, and the heart to do something about it.

THE LORD'S PRAYER.

HYMN: Little drops of water (*DS* 78; *SP* 365).

CLOSING:

Go forth into the world in peace; be of good courage; hold fast that which is good; strengthen the faint-hearted; support the weak; honour all men; love and serve the Lord, rejoicing in the power of the Holy Spirit.
    And the blessing of God Almighty, the Father, the Son, and the Holy Spirit, be upon you, and remain with you always. *Amen.*

BEING ABLE TO WORK

OPENING:

> Teach me, my God and King,
> In all things Thee to see;
> And what I do in anything,
> To do it as for Thee.
> (George Herbert).

THEME:

St. Paul, the great missionary, said: 'We are labourers together with God.' Let us praise God that we are able to work.

PRAYER:

Lord Jesus, it is the beginning of another day and we have work to do. Give us Thy strength to do our work well, and to meet every difficulty with courage and cheerfulness. And may Thy blessing rest upon all that we do throughout this day. *Amen.*

HYMN: In our work and in our play (*DS* 77; *SP* 538).

POETRY READING: *Every Day* (page 133).

STORY LESSON: *The Little Girl who would not Work* (page 164).

HYMN: God has given us work to do (*IP* 44).

UNISON PRAYER:

> *The Prayer of St. Ignatius of Loyola*
> Teach us, good Lord, to serve Thee as Thou deservest.
> To give and not to count the cost.
> To fight and not to heed the wounds.
> To toil and not to seek for rest.
> To labour and not to ask for any reward
> Save that of knowing that we do Thy will. *Amen.*

SILENT PRAYER:

Whatever work is given to us, help us, O God, to do it well and thoroughly whether it be for ourselves or for others.

THE LORD'S PRAYER.

HYMN: The all-day hymn (*DS* 79; *SP* 565).

CLOSING:

May God the Maker of Mankind, help us in our work today and enable us to do His will. *Amen.*

AUTUMN   20   NOVEMBER

MARTINMAS

St. Martin's Day, 11 November

OPENING:

O Jesu, be our morning light
That we may go forth to the fight
With strength renewed, and armour bright.

THEME:

Today is the special day for St. Martin, or Martinmas as it is called. St. Martin was a Roman soldier who became a Christian.

HYMN: Onward, Christian soldiers! (*DS* 139; *SP* 397).

UNISON PRAYER:

The Prayer of Dedication

Jesus, Friend of the friendless; Helper of the poor; Healer of the sick;
Whose life was spent in doing good; Let us follow in Thy footsteps.
Make us strong to do right; Gentle with the weak; And kind to all who are in sorrow;
That we may be like Thee, our Lord and Master. *Amen.*

BIBLE READING: Therefore take up God's armour (Eph. 6. 13–18).

HYMN: I love the Lord who is my strength (*IP* 23).

STORY LESSON: *St. Martin, the Good Soldier* (page 165).

PRAYER:

Give us, O Lord, the strength to do that which is right and always to be faithful and true. May we be strong in the armour of God and may the shield of God defend us. Help us, like St. Martin of old, to become good soldiers of Jesus Christ. *Amen.*

SILENT PRAYER:

Help us, O God, to be true soldiers of Jesus Christ.

THE LORD'S PRAYER.

HYMN: Stand up, stand up, for Jesus (*DS* 141; *SP* 646).
or
Soldiers of Christ, arise (*DS* 85; *SP* 641).

CLOSING:

Put your strength in the Lord and in His mighty power.
Put on all the armour which God provides.
And the blessing of God Almighty, be upon you, and remain with you for ever. *Amen.*

AUTUMN   21   NOVEMBER

WORKING TOGETHER

OPENING:

Jesus said, 'Where two or three are gathered together in my name, there am I in the midst of them.'

THEME:

Today we are gathered together in His Name and He is with us now. Jesus left eleven friends on earth, to work together and to do His will. Let us think how we can work together in His Name.

31

Lord Jesus, who didst call a company of friends together, help us to learn to live as members of a company, to share things, to bear things, to consider other people, and not to shirk the tiresome jobs. We ask it for your sake. *Amen* (OUP).

HYMN: Father we thank Thee for the night (*DS* 146; *SP* 355).

UNISON PRAYER:

O God, bless our school
That, working together
And playing together
We may learn to serve Thee
And to help one another;
For Jesus' sake. *Amen.* (OUP).

BIBLE READING: The seventy-two helpers of Jesus (Luke *10.* 1–7).

HYMN: God has given us work to do (*IP* 44).

STORY LESSON: *The Monastery on the Island* (page 166).

UNISON PRAYER:

Be Thou with us every day,
In our work and in our play,
When we learn and when we pray.
Hear us, Holy Jesus.

Make us brave, without fear,
Make us happy, full of cheer,
Sure that Thou art always near.
Hear us, Holy Jesus.

May we grow from day to day,
Glad to learn each holy way,
Ever ready to obey.
Hear us, Holy Jesus. *Amen.*

THE LORD'S PRAYER.

HYMN: Heavenly Father, may Thy blessing (*DS* 71; *SP* 516).

> Thy world, O Lord, is great and wide,
> We cannot idly stand aside.
> May we be steadfast, strong, and true
> Together, in the work we do. *Amen.*

AUTUMN 22 NOVEMBER

THE JOY OF MUSIC
St. Cecilia's Day, 22 November

OPENING MUSIC: Beethoven's *'Moonlight Sonata'*.

THEME:

22 November is the special day for St. Cecilia, who is the patron saint of music and musicians. Let us praise God for His gift of music.

PRAYER:

O God, our Father, we praise you this morning for the gift of music and for ears to hear the wonderful sounds of great orchestras and simple instruments. We thank you for great composers who have written down their music for all to enjoy and for modern invention that brings it to us again and again. *Amen.*

HYMN: Let all the world in every corner sing (*DS* 99; *SP* 556).

POETRY READING: *The Fairy Flute* (page 134).

HYMN: Sing a glad song to Christ the King (*IP* 38).

STORY LESSON: *The Moonlight Sonata* (page 167).

PRAYER:

A Litany for God's Music
Our thanks to God for ears to hear
The sounds of Nature sweet and clear,
　　(*Together*) *We praise Thee, Heavenly Father.*

33

The song of birds upon the wing
From dawn to dusk their music bring,
 We praise Thee, Heavenly Father.
The sound of bees that work all day
And hum in such a happy way,
 We praise Thee, Heavenly Father.
For gurgling streams and rushing seas
For sighing winds through whisp'ring trees,
 We praise Thee, Heavenly Father.
All Nature's music doth abound
And in God's garden can be found
For, if you listen, you can hear
The voice of God so sweet and clear. *Amen.*

THE LORD'S PRAYER.

HYMN: All people that on earth do dwell (*DS* 1; *SP* 443).

CLOSING:

Children of the heavenly King,
As you journey sweetly sing;
Sing your Saviour's worthy praise,
Glorious in His works and ways.

AUTUMN   23   NOVEMBER

THANKSGIVING

Thanksgiving Day, U.S.A., 23 November

OPENING:

It is a good thing to give thanks unto the Lord and to sing praises unto His name.

THEME:

In the United States of America, the last Thursday of November is kept as a Thanksgiving Day. Let us thank God, this morning, for all His gifts.

PRAYER:

We give Thee thanks, O Lord our God, for all Thy goodness at all times, and in all places, because Thou hast shielded, rescued, helped and guided us all the days of our lives, and brought us unto this hour. We pray and beseech Thee, merciful God, to grant in Thy goodness that we may spend this day without sin and in joyous reverence of Thee. Through Jesus Christ our Lord. *Amen*. (Liturgy of St. Mark).

HYMN: Now thank we all our God (*DS* 23; *SP* 350).
   or
   Let us with a gladsome mind (*DS* 110; *SP* 12).

UNISON PRAYER:
   So many lovely things have we
   To make us thankful, Lord, to Thee.
   Such blessings come with every day;
   O hear us while our thanks we pay.
   It makes us feel so glad to know
   That Thou, Lord God, dost love us so. *Amen*. (REP).

STORY LESSON:

When the Pilgrim Fathers first landed in America, food was very scarce. But from the Red Indians the Pilgrims learnt how to grow corn and the harvest was good. The Pilgrims gave thanks to God and this was the first Thanksgiving Day in America. Here is a story about the Pilgrims and the Red Indians.

The White Feather of Friendship (page 168).

PRAYER:
                    A Litany of Thanksgiving
Almighty God, we lift up our hearts today in thanksgiving
   for the world and all Thy good gifts.
       (*Together*) *We give Thee thanks, O God.*
For the sky above and the earth beneath; for the ever-changing
   seasons and all the wonders of Nature.
               We give Thee thanks, O God.
For our homes and friends, our mothers and fathers and their
   love that surrounds us.
               We give Thee thanks, O God.

35

Above all, for the life and example of Thy Son, Jesus Christ
our Lord, who came on earth to teach us Thy truth.
We give Thee thanks, O God. Amen.

HYMN: We thank you, Lord of Heaven (*DS* 116; *SP* 692).

CLOSING:

> Count your blessings,
> Name them one by one
> And it will surprise you
> What the Lord has done.

AUTUMN   24   NOVEMBER

ADVENT

Feast of St. Andrew, 30 November

OPENING:

> For unto us a child is born
> Unto us a son is given.

THEME:

The last day of November is St. Andrew's Day, and the nearest
Sunday to this day marks the beginning of Advent. Advent means
'coming'—the coming of Jesus. So now we look forward to
Christmas, the birthday of Jesus.

HYMN: Hark the glad sound! the Saviour comes (*DS* 44; *SP* 62).
    or
    O come, O come, Emmanuel! (*DS* 45; *SP* 66).

PRAYER:

O Heavenly Father, we thank you for your gift to the world of
Thy Son, Jesus Christ our Lord. As we think of the coming of
Jesus, help us to make ready a place in our hearts for Him and to
look for Him day by day. *Amen.*

HYMN: Christmas is coming, is coming again (*IP* 58).

Perhaps St. Andrew's Day comes near to Advent because Andrew was one of the first men to follow Jesus. Here is the story of how it happened.

Fishers of Men (page 169).

PRAYER:

> For Jesus, born a little child,
> We thank our Heavenly Father.
> For Jesus, loving, kind and mild,
> We thank our Heavenly Father.
> For Jesus Christ, the children's Friend,
> Who to us all His love doth send,
> For Him Who loves to us the end,
> We thank our Heavenly Father. *Amen.*
> (Carey Bonner).

SILENT PRAYER:

Let us think of all that the coming of Jesus means to us.

THE LORD'S PRAYER.

HYMN: Jesus, good above all other (*DS* 125; *SP* 540).

CLOSING:

Help us, O Lord, always to wait for Thee, to wish for Thee, and to watch for Thee, that at Thy coming again Thou mayest find us ready. *Amen.*

AUTUMN 25 DECEMBER

ST. NICHOLAS

St. Nicholas's Day, 6 December

OPENING:

As we wait the coming of Jesus, let us give thanks to God for the gift of His Son who was born for us in a manger, in a stable at

Bethlehem. May we remember, in His Name to keep the Spirit of Christmastide not just once a year, but for all the days to come.

CAROL: Away in a manger (*IP* 59).

PRAYER:

O holy Jesus, once a little Child for us, help us to remember the Manger at Bethlehem, and always to bring to Thee lowly, loving and grateful hearts. *Amen.*

CAROL: Who within that stable cries (*DS* 43; *SP* 700).

POETRY READING: *What was it like?* (page 134).

THEME:

Today is the special day for St. Nicholas, the patron saint of children. In America the children say a poem which begins:

'Twas the night before Christmas, when all through the house
Not a creature was stirring, not even a mouse;
The stockings were hung by the chimney with care,
In hope that St. Nicholas soon would be there.

STORY LESSON:

Here is a story about St. Nicholas.
The Gifts in the Night (page 170).

PRAYER:

O God, we praise Thee for Thy love to us, and above all for the glad news of the birthday of Jesus. May we, in our carols, sing of our gladness to Thee and by our gifts share Christmas joy with other people. *Amen.*

THE LORD'S PRAYER.

CAROL: When the herds were watching (*DS* 42; *SP* 379).

CLOSING:

Lord Jesus Christ, eternal Child,
Make thou our childhood thine;
That we with Thee the meek and mild
May share the love divine. *Amen.*

THE CHRISTMAS TREE

A Gift from Norway

OPENING:

> Light the candles on the tree,
> Christ was born for you and me.
> Light the candles in the hall,
> He was born to help us all.
> Light the candles up and down,
> In the country and the town.
> Light the candles everywhere,
> He was born a Baby fair.
> (C. Rossetti).

CAROL: Sing a song of candles (*IP* 65).

PRAYER:

Dear Heavenly Father, we think this morning of the Baby Jesus who, for our sakes, was pleased to be born in a stable. We ask you to bless all who are poor and homeless and to make the good news of Thy love for everyone to be known throughout the world. *Amen.*

POETRY READING: *The Little Fir Tree* (page 135).

THEME:

At this time of the year the people of Norway send a gift to the British people—the gift of a Christmas tree. Here is a story about a tree that grew by the inn at Bethlehem.

STORY LESSON: *The First Christmas Tree* (page 171).

PRAYER:

> We thank you for the little Child,
> The Son of God who came to earth.
> To lowly shepherds in the fields
> The Angel Song proclaimed His birth.
> Now we, with them, our thanks we bring
> For Jesus Christ, our Heavenly King. *Amen.*

Let us think, in silence, of the message of goodwill then begun in Bethlehem.

THE LORD'S PRAYER.

CAROLS: From out of a wood did a cuckoo fly
(*DS* 3; Carols; *SP* 381).

CLOSING:

His Name shall be the Prince of Peace
For evermore adored,
The Wonderful, the Counsellor
The great and mighty Lord.

AUTUMN 27 DECEMBER

CHRISTMAS DECORATIONS
Ten Days to Christmas

OPENING:

Deck the hall with boughs of holly,
'Tis the season to be jolly.
Don we now our gay apparel,
Sing the ancient Christmas carol.

THEME:

Of all the evergreens that we use for Christmas decoration, the holly comes first. The name 'holly' comes from an old word meaning 'holy', and Christmas is a holy time.

CAROL: Now the holly bears a berry as white as the milk
(*DS* 8, Carols).

PRAYER:

We praise you, Heavenly Father, for the fun and happiness that Christmas brings each year. As we make our decorations, help us not to be so busy with our own happiness that we forget to make it a happy time for other people. *Amen.*

POETRY READING: *Christmastide* (page 135).

CAROL: Christmas is coming, is coming again (*IP* 58).

STORY LESSON: *The Silver Cones* (page 173).

PRAYER:

> We thank you, Father God, for all the joys of Christmastide,
> For Christmas trees with lights so gay,
> For shining star that led the way,
> For chains and garlands, red and green,
> For all the joyous Christmas scene,
> For carols and the songs we sing,
> As Christmas bells their message ring.
> And now for all Thy gifts we say
> Thank you, Father God, today. *Amen.*

THE LORD'S PRAYER.

CAROL: The holly and the ivy (*Kingsway Carol Book*).

CLOSING:

> Red berries on the picture-frame
> White berries in the hall—
> Let Christmas day look twice as gay
> With evergreens for all.
> (Eleanor Farjeon (Michael Joseph)).

AUTUMN   28   DECEMBER

THE JOURNEY OF MARY AND JOSEPH
Nine Days to Christmas

OPENING:

> How far is it to Bethlehem?
> Not very far.
> Shall we find the stable-room
> Lit by a star?

THEME:

16 December—nine days to Christmas Day. It is believed that Mary and Joseph, travelling slowly with a donkey, would have taken nine days to go from Nazareth to Bethlehem. So, today, in Mexico little children start on a short journey round the village to remember those nine days that Mary and Joseph spent travelling long ago.

CAROL: O little town of Bethlehem (*DS* 50; *SP* 79).

PRAYER:

Dear Loving Father, we remember today the journey of Mary and Joseph on their way to Bethlehem, Help us to think of our mothers and fathers and to thank you for giving us homes of our own and families to which we belong. We ask for Thy blessing on those who are near and dear to us. For Jesus' sake. *Amen.*

BIBLE READING:

And it came to pass in those days, that there went out a decree from Caesar Augustus, that all the world should be taxed . . . And all went to be taxed, every one into his own city. And Joseph also went up from Galilee, out of the city of Nazareth, into Judaea, unto the city of David, which is called Bethlehem . . . to be taxed with Mary his espoused wife. (Luke *2.* 1–5 AV).

STORY LESSON: *The Journey to Bethlehem* (page 172).

PRAYER:

O Lord Jesus, at whose cradle the angels sang, we would join with the angels, the shepherds, and the wise men in the offering of our love and praise. We ask you to accept our prayers and to come and dwell in our hearts for ever. *Amen.*

SILENT PRAYER:

Let us, in silence, thank God for the Baby Jesus.

THE LORD'S PRAYER.

CAROL: Once in royal David's city (*DS* 41; *SP* 368).

> Well may we sing the Saviour's birth
> Who need the grace so given,
> And hail His coming down to earth
> To lift us up to Heaven.

AUTUMN 29 DECEMBER

THE SHEPHERDS IN THE FIELDS

OPENING:

> *At Bethlehem*
> 'What means the star,' the shepherds said,
> 'That brightens through the rocky glen?'
> And angels, answering overhead,
> Said, 'Peace on earth, goodwill to men.'
> (J. R. Lowell.)

BIBLE READING:

Now in this same district there were shepherds out in the fields, keeping watch through the night over their flock, when suddenly there stood before them an angel of the Lord, and the splendour of the Lord shone round them. They were terror-struck, but the angel said, 'Do not be afraid; I have good news for you: there is great joy coming to the whole people. Today in the city of David a deliverer has been born to you—the Messiah, the Lord. And this is your sign: you will find a baby lying all wrapped up, in a manger.' (Luke 2. 8–13 *NEB*).

CAROL: While shepherds watched their flocks by night
(*DS* 47; *SP* 82).

PRAYER:

O Father God, as the shepherds hastened to the manger we would offer our praise and thanks to you this Christmastide. May we rejoice most of all because it is the birthday of the Lord Jesus

43

Christ who was sent by you into the world. Help us to grow more like Him day by day. *Amen.*

POETRY READING: *The Shepherds Slept* (page 136).

STORY LESSON: *The Lonely Shepherd* (page 174).

BIBLE READING:

After the angels had left them and gone into heaven the shepherds said to one another, 'Come, we must go straight to Bethlehem and see this thing that has happened, which the Lord has made known to us.' So they went with all speed and found their way to Mary and Joseph; and the baby was lying in the manger. (Luke 2. 15–17 *NEB*).

CAROL: Jesus, Baby Jesus (*IP* 61).

THE LORD'S PRAYER.

CLOSING:

> Teach, O teach us, Holy Child
> By Thy face so meek and mild.
> Teach us to resemble Thee,
> In Thy sweet humility. *Amen.*

AUTUMN 30 DECEMBER

THE WISE MEN FROM THE EAST
At the Stable

OPENING PRAYER:

O holy Jesus, who led the Wise Men by a star, draw us unto Thee that we may worship, love, and serve Thee for evermore. *Amen.*

BIBLE READING:

Now when Jesus was born in Bethlehem of Judaea in the days of Herod the king, behold, there came wise men from the east to

44

Jerusalem, saying, Where is he that is born King of the Jews? for we have seen his star in the east, and are come to worship him. (Mat. *2.* 1–2 AV.)

CAROL: As with gladness men of old (*DS* 52; *SP* 83).

BIBLE READING:
And, lo, the star, which they saw in the east, went before them, till it came and stood over where the young child was. When they saw the star, they rejoiced with exceeding great joy.

And when they were come into the house, they saw the young child with Mary his mother, and fell down, and worshipped him: and when they had opened their treasures, they presented unto him gifts; gold, and frankincense, and myrrh. (Mat. *2.* 9–11 AV.)

CAROL: Over the hills to Bethlehem (*IP* 66).

POETRY READING: *The Three Kings* (page 136).

STORY LESSON: *Baboushka* (page 175).

PRAYER:
> To Jesus, now the Infant King,
> The wise men came, their gifts to bring;
> Like them, we now before Thee lay
> Our humble gift of love today.
> O show us, Lord, what we can do
> That we may know and serve Thee too. *Amen.*

SILENT PRAYER:
Christmas is the time for giving. God gave us His only Son at Christmastide. Let us think what we can give to others to bring happiness at this time.

THE LORD'S PRAYER.

CAROL: We three kings of Orient are (*DS* 7, Carols).

CLOSING:
> May we live to know and serve Him.
> Trust and love Him all our days,
> Then to dwell for ever near Him,
> See His face and sing His praise.

GIFTS TO THE CHRIST CHILD
At the Manger

OPENING:

> What can I give Him,
> Poor as I am?
> If I were a shepherd
> I would bring a lamb;
> If I were a wise man
> I would do my part;
> Yet what can I give Him—
> Give my heart.
> (Christina Rossetti).

CAROL: A boy was born in Bethlehem (*DS* 2, Carols).

PRAYER: *A Litany for Christmas Time*

For all the joy and happiness of Christmas time,
> (*Together*)   *We give Thee thanks, O God.*
For the fun and laughter of games and parties,
> *We give Thee thanks, O God.*
For the joy of presents we give and for gifts we receive,
> *We give Thee thanks, O God.*
Above all, we thank you for the gift of Thy Son who was born
to us at Bethlehem,
> *We give Thee thanks, O God. Amen.*

CAROL: Rejoice and be merry in songs and in mirth (*DS* 6, Carols).

POETRY READING: *Come away to Bethlehem* (page 137).

THEME:

Today we are thinking of the happiness of gift-making at Christmas time. Here is the story of a gift to Jesus made by a little girl.

STORY LESSON: *The Christmas Rose* (page 176).

PRAYER:

Our Father God, we thank Thee that in the silence of the night Thou didst send Thy Son into the world to be Thy greatest gift and to save us. Help us, now, to be silent and to wait upon Thee; then, in that stillness and silence, may we receive Thy Holy Spirit, so that once again the Lord Jesus may live in our hearts.

PERIOD OF SILENCE.

THE LORD'S PRAYER.

CAROL: Baby Jesus, sleeping softly (*IP* 60).

CLOSING:

Grant us, O God, such love and wonder that with humble shepherds, wise men, and pilgrims unknown, we may come and adore the Holy Babe, the Heavenly King; and with our gifts, worship and serve Him our Lord and Saviour Jesus Christ. *Amen.*

(James Ferguson).

AUTUMN   32   DECEMBER

THE BIRDS AND THE BEASTS KEEP CHRISTMAS

Carol Service

READER:

The Friendly Beasts
Jesus, our brother, kind and good,
Was humbly born in a stable rude,
And the friendly beasts around Him stood;
Jesus, our brother, kind and good.
(Robert Davies).

CAROL: Away in a manger (*IP* 59).

READER:

Jesus was born in a stable because there was no room in the inn at Bethlehem. Around Him were the animals of the field, and above Him the birds flew among the rafters and the doves sat roosting.

FIRST CHILD:

> 'I,' said the dove from the rafters high,
> 'Cooed Him to sleep, that He should not cry,
> We cooed Him to sleep, my mate and I,
> I,' said the dove from the rafters high.

CAROL: The birds (*DS* 3, Carols).

READER:

And in the stable, there was the donkey that had carried Mary, the mother of Jesus, across the hills from Nazareth to Bethlehem.

SECOND CHILD:

> 'I,' said the donkey, shaggy and brown,
> 'I carried His Mother up hill and down;
> I carried her safely to Bethlehem town,
> I,' said the donkey, shaggy and brown.

CAROL: Out in a stable near Bethlehem town (*Kingsway Carol Book*, No. 39).

READER:

And there were shepherds, keeping watch over their flock by night, who hastened to the manger where Jesus lay sleeping.

THIRD CHILD:

> 'I,' said the sheep with curly horn,
> 'I gave Him my wool for His blanket warm,
> He wore my coat on Christmas morn,
> I,' said the sheep with curly horn.

CAROL: Rocking (*Kingsway Carol Book*, No. 28).

READER:

When Jesus was born in Bethlehem, in the days of Herod the king, there came wise men from the east. Riding upon camels across the desert, they followed the star and brought gifts to the Holy Child.

FOURTH CHILD:

'I,' said the camel, yellow and black,
'Over the desert, upon my back
I brought Him gifts in the Wise Men's pack,
I,' said the camel, yellow and black.

CAROL: We three kings of Orient are (*DS* 7, Carols).

READER:

On the night that Jesus was born, a little glow-worm was in the field where the sheep lay sleeping. She had heard the angels singing and had seen the shepherds hasten to the manger. All were bringing gifts to the Christ Child, but the little glow-worm had nothing to offer. All she had was a tiny hayseed that had fallen in the field outside Bethlehem.

'I will take this to the Holy Child,' said the glow-worm, and she set off across the field to the stable. It was a long way for such a tiny creature but, at last, she reached the stable door. She crawled up into the manger and put her gift near to the Baby Jesus.

Although it was such a tiny gift, the Holy Child saw it. Putting out His hand, Jesus touched the little creature who had tried so hard to bring a gift for Him. At once, the glow-worm shone with a soft gentle light—a light that she has carried since the first Christmas Day.

FIFTH CHILD:

Thus every beast by some good spell,
In the stable dark was glad to tell
Of the gift he gave Emmanuel,
The gift he gave Emmanuel.

CAROL: Under Bethlehem's star so bright (*Kingsway Carol Book*, No. 31).

CLOSING PRAYER:

O God our Father, be with us all this Christmastide. Grant that as we keep the birthday of Jesus, He may be born again in our hearts. Take care of those in need and may we remember them amidst our rejoicing. Bless this our Carol Service and show us Jesus as He really is, so that we may think of Him and work for Him, today and every day. *Amen.*

49

THE NEW YEAR
Beginning of the Year

OPENING:

And I said to the man who stood at the gate of the year: Give me a light that I may tread safely into the unknown. And he replied: Go out into the darkness and put your hand into the hand of God. That shall be to you better than light and safer than a known way.
(M. Louise Haskins).

THEME:

As we stand at the gate of the year and the beginning of a new term, let us thank God for all new beginnings and fresh opportunities.

PRAYER:

O Lord our God, we thank you for the bright promise of a New Year. We look forward to the freshness of springtime, the joy of summer holidays, and the many days that will bring their special treasures of happiness. Help us to make this coming year a glad one for other people and to use our time in Thy service. *Amen.*

HYMN: New every morning is the love (*DS* 149; *SP* 31)
or
Lord, behold us with Thy blessing (*DS* 163; *SP* 333).

POETRY READING: *What will the New Year bring?* (page 137).

HYMN: Father, lead me day by day (*IP* 17).

STORY LESSON: *The Twelve Months of the Year* (page 177).

PRAYER:

O God our Father, help us through the coming year to live each day as it comes with strength and courage and a firm resolve to serve Thee in every way, for Jesus' sake. *Amen.* (J. G. Williams).

50

Let us promise that, throughout this coming year, we will follow Jesus in every way.

THE LORD'S PRAYER.

HYMN: Saviour, teach me day by day (*DS* 133; *SP* 370).

CLOSING:

> Whether we mutter a thank you or not,
> We're most of us glad for what we have got;
> So let us today and all through the year
> Thank God with words that are joyful to hear.

SPRING   34   JANUARY

THE BIBLE

A Guide for the Year

OPENING:
Jesus said, 'Blessed are they that hear the word of God, and keep it.'

THEME:
Today we are thinking about the Bible, in which is written the Word of God. In the Psalms is written these words: O God, thy word is a lamp unto my feet, and a light unto my path.

PRAYER:
We thank you, Heavenly Father, for the Bible which is your word to us. We thank you for the wonderful stories of Jesus, our Friend and Saviour. Help us to read and learn and understand, so that we may be like Him. *Amen.*

HYMN: God has given us a book full of stories (*IP* 20).

FIRST BIBLE READING: A sower went out to sow (Mark *4*. 3–9 *NEB*).

HYMN: We love the wonderful stories (*Children Praising*, No. 53, OUP).

SECOND BIBLE READING: Jesus explains the parable (Mark *4*. 10, 13–20 *NEB*).

STORY LESSON:

Once upon a time, Bibles were very expensive and few people could read them. Today, there are Bibles all over the world sent by the British and Foreign Bible Society—and this is how it all began.

A Bible for Mary (page 178).

PRAYER:

A Litany for the Bible

For all the praise and teaching of the Bible,
> (*Together*) *We thank Thee, Heavenly Father.*
For Thy servants of old who suffered hardship and danger
to write down Thy Holy Word,
> *We thank Thee, Heavenly Father.*
For the wonderful books of the Old Testament and the
stories about the prophets of old,
> *We thank Thee, Heavenly Father.*
For the New Learning in the New Testament that Jesus has
given to us and for the story of His Life on earth,
> *We thank Thee, Heavenly Father.*
Give us true understanding of Thy Word, O Lord, that we
may grow in grace and in knowledge of our Lord and
Saviour, Jesus Christ. *Amen.*

THE LORD'S PRAYER.

HYMN: There is a book who runs may read (*DS* 27; *SP* 664).

CLOSING:

Lord, teach me all that I should know;
In grace and wisdom may I grow;
The more I learn to do Thy Will,
The better may I love Thee still. *Amen.*

(Isaac Watts).

WINTERTIME
January Days

OPENING:

Out of the south cometh the whirlwind: And cold out of the north. [And] By the breath of God frost is given. (Job *37. 9.*).

THEME:

In these wintry days of the New Year, let us thank God our Father for His gift of wintertime.

PRAYER:

We thank you, Heavenly Father, for the beauty of wintertime, with snow on the hills and frost in the air. We thank you for this time when seeds and roots are safely asleep in the earth, to waken again in the days of Spring. *Amen.*

HYMN: Winter creeps, nature sleeps (*DS* 117; *SP* 380).

POETRY READING: *White World* (page 138).

HYMN: Little birds in wintertime (*Child Songs*, No. 39).

STORY LESSON: *Why the Owl is Cold* (page 180).

PRAYER:

Our praise and thanks to Thee we bring,
For wintertime upon the earth,
When all Thy gifts of buds and flowers
Await the sun to give them birth.

For glowing fires to keep us warm,
When frost is on the window pane.
All seasons shall be sweet to Thee,
For Thou wilt send the Spring again. *Amen.*

THE LORD'S PRAYER.

HYMN: For the beauty of the earth (*DS* 113; *SP* 494).

O God! who giv'st the winter's cold,
As well as summer's joyous rays
Us warmly in Thy love enfold,
And keep us through life's wintry days.
(S. Longfellow).

SPRING 36 JANUARY

THE GOOD SHEPHERD

OPENING:

Jesus said, 'I am the good shepherd and know my sheep and am known of mine. My sheep hear my voice, and I know them and they follow me, and I will give unto them eternal life and they shall never perish neither shall any man pluck them out of my hand.'

THEME:

Today, we are thinking of God's love and care for us all, which is like that of a shepherd caring for each one of his flock.

HYMN: The King of love my Shepherd is (*DS* 28; *SP* 654).

PRAYER:

O Lord Jesus, who art the great Shepherd of the sheep, help us to walk in Thy footsteps day by day. Give us grace to follow where Thou dost lead, so that we may be enfolded in the love of Thy flock for ever. *Amen.*

BIBLE READING: The Lord is my Shepherd; I shall not want (Psa. *23*).

HYMN: Father, lead me day by day (*IP* 17).

STORY LESSON: *The Shepherd with a Hundred Sheep* (page 181).

PRAYER:

> The Lord our pasture shall prepare
> And feed us with a shepherd's care;
> His presence shall our wants supply
> And guard us with a watchful eye;
> Our daily needs He shall attend
> And us from danger will defend.
>
> *Amen.*

SILENT PRAYER:

Help us, O Lord, to follow you at all times.

THE LORD'S PRAYER.

HYMN: The Lord's my Shepherd, I'll not want (*DS* 214) (Crimond).

CLOSING:

Now the God of peace, that brought again from the dead our Lord Jesus Christ, that great Shepherd of the sheep, make us perfect in every good work to do His will—through Jesus Christ, our Lord, to whom be glory for ever and ever. *Amen.*

SPRING　　　37　　　JANUARY

CARE OF THE SICK

OPENING:

God is our refuge and our strength, a very present help in time of trouble.

THEME:

Jesus was always ready to help those who were hurt or ill, and we must try to be like Him. Let us pray for sick people everywhere—in hospital or at home.

PRAYER:

Our Father God, we know that Thy Son Jesus Christ went about doing good and healing all kinds of sickness among the people.

55

Help us to be kind like Him and to remember those who are ill today. Send down Thy blessing on all doctors and nurses who work to prevent suffering and so follow the loving kindness of our Lord Jesus Christ. *Amen.*

HYMN: Thine arm, O Lord, in days of old (*DS* 159; *SP* 287).

BIBLE READING: Jesus cures the son of a nobleman (John *4.* 46–53 *NEB*).

HYMN: For all the strength we have (*IP* 31).

STORY LESSON: *St. Roche and his Little Dog* (page 182).

PRAYER:

Lord Jesus, who didst heal and bless
The sick, and all in pain.
Look down upon the sick today,
And make them well again.

For all the health and strength we have,
Our thanks to you we pray,
May we be quick to help the sick,
Today and every day. *Amen.*

SILENT PRAYER:

Let us think about those who are suffering and ask God to make them well again.

THE LORD'S PRAYER.

HYMN: Jesus' hands were kind hands doing good to all (*IP* 70).

CLOSING:

Now unto God, the giver of all life, and to His Son Jesus Christ, who came that we might have life more abundantly, be all honour and glory, world without end. *Amen.*

MISSIONS AND MISSIONARIES
Conversion of St. Paul, 25 January

OPENING:

Jesus said, 'But there are other sheep of mine, not belonging to this fold, whom I must bring in; and they too will listen to my voice. There will then be one flock, one shepherd.'

THEME:

On 25 January the Church remembers how St. Paul became a Christian. St. Paul was one of the first great Christian missionaries. Let us, today, think of those who work for the Church abroad.

PRAYER:

We bring to Thee in prayer, O God, all missionaries who have left their homes to go to distant lands. Protect them in all their dangers and help them in all their difficulties, so that they may never be lonely or afraid, because Thou art with them. For Jesus Christ's sake. *Amen.*

HYMN: Remember all the people (*DS* 140; *SP* 369).

BIBLE READING: Make all nations my disciples (Mat. *28.* 16–20 *NEB*).

HYMN: Over the sea there are little brown children (*IP* 11).

STORY LESSON: *Paul, the Great Missionary* (page 183).

PRAYER:

For all who spread the Good News

We praise thy Name, O God, for all who have spread the good news of the Gospel throughout the world,
(*Together*) *We praise Thee, O God.*
For all who have braved the perils of the deep and the dangers of untrodden paths and unknown peoples,
We praise Thee, O God.

For all who have worked to free the slave and heal the
sick,
We praise Thee, O God.
For all Thy servants who have left their homes to labour
overseas, we praise Thy Holy Name. *Amen.*

THE LORD'S PRAYER.

HYMN: In Christ there is no East or West (*DS* 210; *SP* 537).

CLOSING:

O Thou, who didst command Thy Apostles to go into all the world,
and to preach the Gospel to everyone; let Thy Name be great
among all nations, from the rising up of the sun unto the going
down of the same. *Amen.*

SPRING   39   JANUARY

BEING HONEST

OPENING HYMN: Heavenly Father, may thy blessing (*DS* 71; *SP* 516).

BIBLE READING: Zaccheus meets Jesus (Luke *19.* 1–10 *NEB*).

THEME:

Whatsoever things are true, whatsoever things are honest, think
on these things. Zaccheus was a cheat, yet he was forgiven by
Jesus. Let us pray for truth and honesty.

PRAYER:

Lord, grant us the strength to do in all things that which is honest
and right. Help us bravely to speak the truth and to behave
openly and honestly. May we never be afraid to say that we are
wrong or to take the blame. We ask it for Thy Name's sake. *Amen.*

HYMN: Father, lead me day by day (*IP* 17).

POETRY READING: *Four Things* (page 138).

STORY LESSON: *The Greasy Cakes* (page 184).

PRAYER:

> Dear God, I like to think
> Of Jesus, who came that we might know:
> Help us in all our work and play
> To do our best in every way,
> And so, like Him to grow. *Amen.*

SILENT PRAYER:

Give us, O Lord, the wisdom and strength to fight against things which we know to be wrong.

THE LORD'S PRAYER.

HYMN: Lead us, heavenly Father, lead us (*DS* 206; *SP* 555).

CLOSING:

Almighty God, grant unto us who know that we are weak, and who trust in thee because we know that thou art strong, the gladsome help of thy loving-kindness, through Jesus Christ our Lord. *Amen.* (*Roman Breviary*).

SPRING   40   JANUARY

THE LISTENING HEART

OPENING:

> High up, away on a great hill,
> Jesus was praying, kneeling still;
> There was no movement and no sound,
> But the low wind that breathed around;
> Lord Jesus, keep me very still,
> With you upon your lonely hill. (SCM).

THEME:

In the Bible we are told that God often spoke to those who would listen. He spoke to Jacob at Bethel, to Elijah in the desert, and to the boy Samuel in the temple. Let us pray for a 'listening heart'.

PRAYER:

In the quiet of our hearts Thou dost speak to us day by day with Thy voice so gentle and so still. Teach us, O Lord, to have listening hearts, so that we may not miss the faintest whisper of Thy Voice helping us to do what is right. Help us, like Samuel, to listen and to answer, 'Speak Lord, for Thy servant heareth.' *Amen.* (CSSM.)

HYMN: Breathe on me, breath of God (*DS* 88; *SP* 458).

POETRY READING: *The Voice of God* (page 139).

HYMN: Loving Shepherd, ever near (*IP* 28).

STORY LESSON: *The Calling of Samuel* (page 186).

PRAYER:

> Speak, Lord! and from our earliest days
> Incline our hearts to love Thy ways:
> Thy waking voice hath reach'd our ear,
> Speak Lord to us, Thy servants hear. *Amen.*
> (Ann Taylor)

SILENT PRAYER:

Let us be quiet and listen for the voice of God today.

THE LORD'S PRAYER.

HYMN: My God, how wonderful thou art (*DS* 8; *SP* 581).

CLOSING:

O Lord Jesus Christ, be pleased today and every day to walk with my feet and work with my hands, to see with my eyes and to hear with my ears, to think with my mind and to speak with my lips, and to love with my heart, that I may be useful and happy in Thy service. *Amen.*

A LIGHT FOR ALL THE WORLD

Candlemas, 2 February

OPENING:

Jesus said, 'I am the light of the world. No follower of mine shall wander in the dark; he shall have the light of life.'

THEME:

On this day we remember when Jesus, as a baby, was taken to the Temple in Jerusalem. This day is also called Candlemas because, in olden times, candles were lit in the churches to remind people that Jesus was 'a light to lighten the Gentiles.'

PRAYER:

O Lord our Heavenly Father, we ask this morning that you will drive away all darkness from our hearts, and bring us to the true Light of the World, Jesus Christ our Lord. *Amen.*

HYMN: Jesus bids us shine with a pure clear light (*IP* 49).

BIBLE READING:

You are light for all the world. A town that stands on a hill cannot be hidden. When a lamp is lit, it is not put under the meal-tub, but on the lamp-stand, where it gives light to everyone in the house. And you, like the lamp, must shed light among your fellows, so that, when they see the good you do, they may give praise to your Father in heaven. (Mat. *5*, 14–16 *NEB*).

STORY LESSON: *The Gift of Light* (page 187).

PRAYER:

Great God, so holy and so high,
Who filled the dark world full of light;
Help me to feel Thee always nigh,
Though Thou art hidden from my sight.

61

O let me hear Thy loving voice
Deep in my heart, when all is still;
That in the dark I may rejoice,
And learn to know and do Thy Will. *Amen.*

SILENT PRAYER:
Grant, O Lord, that we may live in Thy light, and so bring light
to those in darkness.

THE LORD'S PRAYER.

HYMN: Immortal, invisible, God only wise (*DS* 6; *SP* 535).

CLOSING:
There shall be no night there, where we shall be for ever with the
Lord; and here also, if we follow Him, we shall not walk in
darkness, but have the Light of Life. Let Thy peace, O Lord, be
with us both now and for evermore. *Amen.* (*A Chain of Prayer
Across the Ages*).

SPRING 42 FEBRUARY

FINDING JESUS

OPENING:
Jesus said, 'Ask and you will receive; seek, and you will find;
knock, and the door will be opened.'

THEME:
The disciple Thomas once said to Jesus, 'Lord, we do not know
where you are going, so how can we know the way?'
Jesus replied, 'I am the way. . . the truth . . . and the life. No
man comes to the Father except by me. If you knew me you would
know my Father too.'

The Prayer of Dedication

Jesus, Friend of the friendless;
Helper of the poor; Healer of the sick;
Whose life was spent in doing good; Let us follow in Thy footsteps.
Make us strong to do right; Gentle with the weak;
And kind to all who are in sorrow; That we may be like Thee;
Our Lord and Master. *Amen.*

HYMN: Jesus, friend of little children (*SP* 363; *IP* 26).

POETRY READING: *Just for Jesus* (page 139).

STORY LESSON: *Martin, the Cobbler* (page 188).

PRAYER:

Loving Jesus, gentle Lamb,
In Thy gracious hands I am.
Make me, Saviour, what thou art,
Live thyself within my heart.

I shall then show forth thy praise,
Serve thee all my happy days;
Then the world shall always see
Christ, the Holy Child, in me. *Amen.*
(Chas. Wesley).

SILENT PRAYER:

Let us think, in silence, how we can find Jesus today by helping others.

THE LORD'S PRAYER.

HYMN: Jesus, good above all other (*DS* 125; *SP* 540).

CLOSING:

The grace of our Lord Jesus Christ, and the love of God and the fellowship of the Holy Spirit, be with us all—now and for evermore. *Amen.*

BEING GRATEFUL

OPENING:

All good giving and every perfect gift comes from above, from the Father of the lights of Heaven.

THEME:

Let us, this morning, be grateful for the good things around us and give thanks unto the Lord.

HYMN: We thank you, Lord of Heaven (*DS* 116; *SP* 692).

UNISON PRAYER:

O Father of goodness
We thank Thee each one
For happiness and healthiness,
Friendship and fun;
For good things we think of
And good things we do;
And all that is beautiful,
Loving and true. *Amen.*

HYMN: Thank you, God, for all you give us (*IP* 42).

BIBLE READING: The grateful leper (Luke *17*. 11–19 *NEB*).

STORY LESSON: *The Juggler in the Monastery* (page 189).

PRAYER:

Give us always thankful hearts, O Lord, for all Thy goodness and loving-kindness to us; above all for Thy love in sending Jesus Christ our Lord to be the Saviour of the world. Help us to remember that everything we have comes to us from Thee, so that our hearts may always be thankful and that we may praise Thee, not only with our lips, but in our lives, by giving ourselves to Thy service, and by walking with Thee day by day. Through Jesus Christ our Lord. *Amen.* (CSSM).

However few our gifts may seem, grant us, O Lord to be willing to lay them at Thy feet.

THE LORD'S PRAYER.

HYMN: Now thank we all our God (*DS* 23; *SP* 350).

CLOSING:

> May the thoughts of our minds
> And the love of our hearts
> And the gifts of our hands
> Be acceptable unto Thee,
> Our God and King. *Amen.*

SPRING 44 FEBRUARY

ST. VALENTINE

St. Valentine's Day, 14 February

OPENING:
Truly the light is sweet and a pleasant thing it is for the eye to behold the sun.
Let us thank God for the gift of sight and for the joy of seeing.

PRAYER:
O Lord, our Heavenly Father, from whom cometh every good and perfect gift, we thank Thee for the precious gift of sight. Teach us to see the beauty of the world around us, and may we not have unseeing eyes for the wonders of Thy kingdom. *Amen.*

HYMN: I often think of God (*IP* 8).

BIBLE READING: Blind Bartimaeus (Mark *10*. 46–52).

HYMN: Thine arm, O Lord, in days of old (*DS* 159; *SP* 287).

PRAYER:

> Praise to God, for things we see,
> The growing flower, the waving tree,
> Our mother's face, the bright blue sky
> Where birds and clouds come floating by,
> Praise to God for seeing. *Amen.*

THEME:

In the month of February comes the special day for St. Valentine. Let us hear how he cured a little blind girl and gave her back her sight.

STORY LESSON: *St. Valentine and the Blind Girl* (page 190).

PRAYER:

> Teach me, my God and King,
> In all things Thee to see;
> And what I do in anything,
> To do it as for Thee. *Amen.*
> (Geo. Herbert).

THE LORD'S PRAYER.

HYMN: Can you count the stars that brightly (*DS* 19; *SP* 462).

CLOSING:

> Gracious Father, grant Thy blessing
> To Thy children waiting still.
> May we all, Thy strength possessing,
> Learn to do Thy holy will. *Amen.*

SPRING 45 FEBRUARY

HELPING OTHERS

Order of St. John, 15 February

OPENING:

Jesus said, 'Thou shalt love the Lord thy God with all thy heart, and with all thy soul, and with all thy strength, and with all thy mind; and . . . thou shalt love thy neighbour as thyself.'

PRAYER:

Almighty and most merciful Father, who hast given us a new commandment that we should love one another, give us also grace that we may fulfil it. Make us gentle, courteous, and forbearing. Direct our lives so that we may look each to the good of others in word and deed. And hallow all our friendships by the blessing of thy Spirit, for his sake who loved us and gave himself for us, Jesus Christ our Lord. *Amen.* (Bishop Westcott).

HYMN: I have a clear message from Jesus, my King (*IP* 48).

UNISON PRAYER:

The Prayer of Dedication

Jesus, Friend of the friendless; Helper of the poor; Healer of the sick; Whose life was spent in doing good; Let us follow in Thy footsteps. Make us strong to do right; Gentle with the weak; And kind to all who are in sorrow; That we may be like Thee, our Lord and Master. *Amen.*

THEME:

'Jesus, Friend of the friendless.' . . . Many people have tried to live up to these words and it was in the month of February that the Order of St. John was started. It began, many years ago, as a band of people who tried to help those who were friendless or in sorrow. First of all, they helped pilgrims to the Holy Land who were hurt or in need. But they also helped anyone, not only pilgrims, as this story from their history shows.

STORY LESSON: *The Dog Brother* (page 191).

HYMN: O dear and lovely Brother (*DS* 37; *SP* 367).

UNISON PRAYER:

Lord of the loving heart, may mine be loving too.
Lord of the gentle hands, may mine be gentle too.
Lord of the willing feet, may mine be willing too.
So may I grow, more like to Thee,
In all I say and do. *Amen.*

CLOSING:

The Lord guide us and bless us and those we love, now and always. *Amen.*

FORGIVING OTHERS

OPENING:

> Jesus said, 'Love your enemies; do good to those who hate you
> . . . treat others as you would like them to treat you.'

THEME:

> Let us pray this morning for strength to forgive others when they
> have done wrong to us.

PRAYER:

> O God, our loving Father, we ask you to give us the forgiving
> spirit. May we never bear a grudge or try to pay back evil for
> evil. Teach us to love one another and forgive us our trespasses—
> as we forgive them that trespass against us. *Amen.*

HYMN: Heavenly Father, may Thy blessing (*DS* 71; *SP* 516).

BIBLE READING: On forgiveness (Mat. *18.* 21–35 *NEB*).

HYMN: For the things that I've done wrong (*IP* 53).

STORY LESSON: *The Silver Candlesticks* (page 192).

PRAYER:

> *The Prayer for Forgiveness*
>
> O God our heavenly Father, forgive us for all our faults remem-
> bered and forgotten. For the things we ought to have done and
> have not done; for the things we have done which have brought
> sorrow to ourselves and others. And as we pray, ourselves, to be
> forgiven, help us to forgive those who have done wrong to us;
> through Jesus Christ our Lord. *Amen.* (DS).

SILENT PRAYER:

> Let us be quiet and remember that today we will forgive those
> who are unkind or forgetful.

THE LORD'S PRAYER.

CLOSING:

Grant, Almighty God, that we may follow Thy commandment
to love one another and so obey Thy Holy Will, through Jesus
Christ our Lord. *Amen.*

SPRING   47   FEBRUARY

THE SEASON OF LENT

Lenten Days

THEME:

This time of the Christian year is called by the name of Lent.
Beginning with Ash Wednesday, it lasts for forty days and ends at
Eastertide, when Jesus died on the cross and rose again.

Many people, during these weeks, go without things they like
to remind them that Jesus fasted in the wilderness for forty days
—and to strengthen themselves against temptation.

HYMN: Through the night thy angels kept (*SP* 375).

PRAYER:

O Lord our heavenly Father, Almighty and everlasting God, who
hast safely brought us to the beginning of this day: Defend us in
the same with Thy mighty power; and grant that this day we fall
into no sin, neither run into any kind of danger; but that all our
doings may be ordered by Thy governance, to do always that
which is righteous in Thy sight; through Jesus Christ our Lord.
Amen. (Prayer Book).

BIBLE READING: The temptations of Jesus (Mat. *4.* 1–11 *NEB*).

STORY LESSON: *John the Baptist* (page 194).

UNISON PRAYER:

> Help me, O God, throughout this day,
> To be kind and fair
> To all with whom I work and play.
> Help me, O God, now day has come,
> To bring joy and love to everyone. *Amen.*

THE LORD'S PRAYER.

HYMN: Fight the good fight with all thy might (*DS* 69; *SP* 491).

CLOSING:

> Lord, help me by Thy grace to be
> Lowly and kind of heart like Thee;
> Gentle and loving, meek and mild,
> Thy servant, though a little child. *Amen.*
>
> (Isaac Watts).

SPRING 48 FEBRUARY

BEING UNSELFISH

Lenten Days

OPENING:

Jesus said, 'Happiness lies more in giving than in receiving.'

THEME:

Let us praise God for the joy of giving and to ask that we may be unselfish, for Jesus has said: 'Give when you are asked to give.'

> Help me, Jesus, to be generous,
> To give away sometimes the things I like,
> The larger share, the better part.
> Help me to give up my pleasures
> If so I give for others a greater good.
> Thou didst lay down Thy life for me,
> So I must spend my life for Thee.
> Let me not think only of myself.
> Let me care for all who are dear to Thee. *Amen.*
> (Father Roche).

HYMN: Jesus, Lord, we look to Thee (*DS* 126; *SP* 541).

BIBLE READING: The Widow's Mite (Mark *12.* 41–44 *NEB*).

HYMN: We pray thee, Father, to accept (*IP* 52).

STORY LESSON: *The Legend of the Woodpecker* (page 195).

PRAYER:

O God, who loves a cheerful giver, help us to find happiness in the things that we can do for each other. May we always remember to give a helping hand to those in need and teach us that the joy of giving is the real joy of living. Through Jesus Christ, who gave Himself for us. *Amen.*

SILENT PRAYER:

Lord, give us faith when we pray, and make all our prayers unselfish.

THE LORD'S PRAYER.

HYMN: Here we come with gladness (*IP* 51).

CLOSING:

Above all, be generous to one another. Whatever gift each of you may have received, use it in service to one another. Give it as in the strength which God supplies. *Amen.* (1 Peter *4*; adapted)

ST. DAVID

St. David's Day, 1 March

THEME:

Today is the special day for St. David, the patron saint of Wales. Let us sing, this morning, the great Welsh melody 'Cwm Rhondda'.

HYMN: Guide me, O thou great Redeemer (*DS* 204).

STORY LESSON: *St. David and the Robbers* (page 196).

PRAYER:

Prayer for St. David's Day

O God, who in Thy providence didst choose Thy servant David to be the apostle of the Welsh people, that he might guide Thy people by his example: Grant us to keep the faith which he taught and to follow in his footsteps, through Jesus Christ our Lord. *Amen.*

THE LORD'S PRAYER.

BIBLE READING:

Here is a story of how another David, the shepherd boy of the Bible, was chosen to be King of Israel. God had sent Samuel to Bethlehem, where the chief man was Jesse, a farmer with eight sons. David is chosen to be king (1 Sam. *16.* 11–13).

HYMN:

Here is another Welsh melody for St. David's Day:

Can you count the stars that brightly (*DS* 19; *SP* 462).

CLOSING:

Almighty and everlasting God, who didst light the flame of love in the heart of St. David, grant to us the same faith and power of love, that as we remember him this day, we may follow his example, through Jesus Christ, our Lord. *Amen.*

MARCH WINDS
March Days

OPENING:
> He caused an east wind to blow in the heaven: and by his power
> he brought in the south wind. (Psa. *78*. 26.).

THEME:
> March is supposed to be the stormy month of strong winds. But an
> old rhyme says 'March winds and April showers, bring forth May
> flowers'. Here is a poem about the wind by Robert Louis
> Stevenson.

POETRY READING: *The Wind* (page 139).

HYMN: Who has seen the wind? (*SP* 386 (III)).

PRAYER:
> Dear Father God, Maker of the beautiful world, we thank you for
> the changing seasons and the never ending strength of Nature.
> We think, today, of the winds of heaven that send the clouds sailing
> across the sky, moving the seas, and spreading Thy seed upon the
> earth. For all Thy gifts to mankind, we give Thee thanks, O God.
> *Amen.*

HYMN: All things bright and beautiful (*DS* 17; *SP* 444).

STORY LESSON: *The Wind and the Sun* (page 197).

BIBLE READING:
> Jesus said: 'The wind blows where it wills; you hear the sound of
> it, but you do not know where it comes from, or where it is going.
> So with everyone who is born from spirit.' (John *3*. 8 *NEB*).

PRAYER:
> For sun and moon and stars:
> Praise be to God.
> For wind and clouds and rain:
> Praise be to God.

For sea and hills and fields:
Praise to be God.
For men and beasts and birds:
Praise be to God. *Amen.*
(Bertha C. Krall).

THE LORD'S PRAYER.

HYMN: All creatures of our God and King (vv. 1 and 2). (*DS* 16; *SP* 439).

CLOSING:

May we remember, throughout this day, how great is God Almighty, Who has made all things well. *Amen.*

SPRING 51 MARCH

PARENTS
Mothering Sunday

OPENING:

Honour thy father and thy mother: that thy days may be long upon the land which the Lord thy God giveth thee. (Exod. *20.* 12).

THEME:

The Sunday which falls in the middle of Lent is called Mothering Sunday. On this day, children and older people remember to say 'Thank you' to their mothers, and take them some gift, such as flowers. Let us thank God for happy homes and kind parents.

PRAYER:

O Lord, our Heavenly Father, we ask for Thy blessing on our homes and families. We thank you for our mothers and fathers and all those who love us and take care of us. Help us to try and

74

help them and grant that we may all love and serve Thee more and more. Through Jesus Christ our Lord. *Amen.*

HYMN: In our work and in our play (*DS* 77; *SP* 538).

POETRY READING: *Mother's Hands* (page 140).

HYMN: Thank you for my mother dear (*IP* 40).

BIBLE READING: The boy Jesus visits Jersualem (Luke 2. 41–47; 51–52 *NEB*).

STORY LESSON: *Two Stories* (page 198).

UNISON PRAYER:

> Dear Heavenly Father,
> Thank you for taking care of us
> Through the night.
> Help us to please you
> All day long.
> May we learn to help one another
> And those at home.
> Bless our fathers and mothers
> And all children all over the world:
> For Thy sake. *Amen.*

SILENT PRAYER:

Let us think, in silence . . . What can I do to make my home a happy place in which to live?

THE LORD'S PRAYER.

HYMN: My God, how wonderful Thou art (*DS* 8; *SP* 581).

CLOSING:

May God, the Father of us all, watch over those whom we love and those who love us, now and for evermore. *Amen.*

ST. PATRICK

St. Patrick's Day, 17 March

THEME:

Today is the special day for St. Patrick, the patron saint of Ireland.
The prayers this morning are the prayers written by St. Patrick.

PRAYER:

> I bind unto myself today
> The power of God to hold and lead;
> His eye to watch, his might to stay,
> His ear to hearken to my need;
> The wisdom of my God to teach,
> His hand to guide, his shield to ward,
> The word of God to give me speech,
> His heavenly host to be my guide. *Amen.*

HYMN:

Here is an ancient Irish hymn melody:

> The King of love my Shepherd is (*DS* 28; *SP* 644).

BIBLE READING:

> I will lift up mine eyes unto the hills,
> From whence cometh my help.
> My help cometh from the Lord,
> Which made heaven and earth. (Psa. *121*).

STORY LESSON: *The Christian Fire* (page 199).

PRAYER:

> Christ be with me, Christ within me,
> Christ behind me, Christ before me.
> Christ beside me, Christ to win me,
> Christ to comfort and restore me.
> Christ beneath me, Christ above me,
> Christ in quiet, Christ in danger.
> Christ in hearts of all that love me,
> Christ in mouth of friend and stranger. *Amen.*

Let us ask, like St. Patrick, for the strength of God to uphold us today.

THE LORD'S PRAYER:

HYMN:

Here is another Irish traditional melody:
O Son of man, our hero strong and tender (*DS* 40; *SP* 611).

CLOSING:

May the strength of God pilot us,
May the power of God preserve us,
May the wisdom of God instruct us, and
May the hand of God protect us; now and for evermore. *Amen.*

SPRING   53   MARCH

SONGS OF PRAISE

Hymn Service

OPENING:

O sing unto the Lord a new song: sing unto the Lord, all the earth.
For the Lord is great, and greatly to be praised. (Psa. *96*).

THEME:

Today we are going to have a Hymn Service. Let us lift up our voices and sing praises to God.

HYMN: O worship the King (vv. 1, 2, and 5) (*DS* 11; *SP* 618).

HYMN:

The next hymn was written by a boy. Millions of people have sung it during the last 300 years and it was written by John Milton when he was only 15 years old:

Let us with a gladsome mind (*DS* 110; *SP* 12).

STORY LESSON: *The Song in the Night* (page 201).

Once a young man was sitting for a mathematics examination. He had finished all the problems but had to stay in the room, so on the back of his examination paper he wrote the first ten lines of a new hymn:

Oft in danger, oft in woe (*DS* 84; *SP* 619).

When Isaac Watts was a little boy, he was very good at 'making up' poems. When he grew up and became a minister, he wrote over 500 hymns and this is one of them:

Jesus shall reign where'er the sun (*DS* 138; *SP* 545).

THE LORD'S PRAYER.

HYMN:

Many years ago, Sunday school children in a village in Yorkshire, used to march round the parish on Whit-Monday singing hymns. The new vicar thought of a good marching tune and wrote these words.

Onward, Christian soldiers! (*DS* 139; *SP* 397).

CLOSING:

O Father, give us grace and sense
To know what we should do,
And then a loving heart, O Lord,
To sing the whole day through. *Amen.*
(Chas. and Mary Lamb).

SPRING 54 MARCH

ST. CUTHBERT

St. Cuthbert's Day, 20 March

OPENING:

Jesus said, 'You did not choose me: I chose you . . . so that the Father may give you all that you ask in my name.' (John *15*. 16. *NEB*).

Today is the special day for St. Cuthbert, one of the three great English saints of the Middle Ages. Here is a prayer for St. Cuthbert's Day.

PRAYER:

Almighty God, we remember today your faithful servant St. Cuthbert. We remember that he was a shepherd and followed the call to spread the Good News of Jesus, that great Shepherd of the sheep. *Amen.*

HYMN: Loving Shepherd of thy sheep (*IP* 28; *SP* 366).

PRAYER:

Lord, as we go to our work this day, help us to take pleasure in all that we do. Show us clearly what our duty is and help us to be faithful in doing it. May all we do be well done, fit for thine eye to see. For Thy Name's sake. *Amen.*

STORY LESSON: *St. Cuthbert and the Eagle* (page 202).

THE LORD'S PRAYER.

BIBLE READING:

Here is a story from the Bible of how Elijah was fed by the ravens.

And the word of the Lord came unto him, saying, Get thee hence, and turn thee eastward, and hide thyself by the brook Cherith, that is before Jordan. And it shall be, that thou shalt drink of the brook; and I have commanded the ravens to feed thee there. So he went and did according unto the word of the Lord: for he went and dwelt by the brook Cherith, that is before Jordan. And the ravens brought him bread and flesh in the morning, and bread and flesh in the evening; and he drank of the brook. (1 Kings *17*. 2–6).

HYMN: The King of love my Shepherd is (*DS* 28; *SP* 654).

CLOSING:

In this hour of the day fill us, O Lord, with thy grace, that rejoicing throughout the whole day we may take delight in thy praise; through Jesus Christ our Lord. *Amen.* (*Sarum Breviary.*)

79

SPRING FLOWERS
First Day of Spring, 21 March

OPENING:

For, lo, the winter is past, the rain is over and gone; the flowers appear on the earth, the time of the singing of birds is come, and the voice of the dove is heard in our land. (Song of Solomon 2. 11–12).

THEME:

In the third week of March comes the first day of Spring, when we are thankful for flowers upon the earth and the miracle of Springtime.

PRAYER:

We thank you, Heavenly Father, for all the loveliness of spring and the wakening of the earth after its winter sleep. We thank you for the beauty of spring flowers and their many colours, for their wonderful shapes and perfect patterns and for the promise that new life is about to begin. *Amen.*

HYMN: Daisies are our silver (*DS* 112; *SP* 354).

POETRY READING: *Spring* (page 140).

HYMN: We thank thee, heavenly Father (*IP* 87).

Story Lesson: *The Angel of the Flowers* (page 200).

PRAYER:

We thank you for the flowers so sweet,
That spread a carpet at our feet:
The tint upon the smallest rose,
The shape of everything that grows.

We thank you for the lilies tall
That grow against the garden wall,
The bluebell and the daffodil
And flowers wild upon the hill.

That tint upon the smallest rose,
That shape of everything that grows,
Thy hand, O God, has placed it there,
Thy work, O God, is everywhere. *Amen.*

THE LORD'S PRAYER.

HYMN: For the beauty of the earth (*DS* 113; *SP* 494).

CLOSING:

The ever changing seasons
In silence come and go;
But thou, eternal Father,
No time or change canst know. *Amen.*

SPRING 56 MARCH

BEING KIND

THEME:

St. Paul once wrote these words in a letter: Be ye kind one to
another, tenderhearted, forgiving one another, even as God for
Christ's sake hath forgiven you.

PRAYER:

Great God! Forgive, whenever we
Forget Thy will and disagree;
And grant that each of us may find
The sweet delight of being kind. *Amen.*
(Ann Taylor, 1782–1866).

HYMN: Jesus' hands were kind hands, doing good to all (*IP* 70).

PRAYER:

Grant, O Lord, that in all the joys of life we may never forget to
be kind. Help us to be unselfish in Friendship, thoughtful of those
less happy than ourselves, and eager to bear the burdens of others:
through Jesus Christ our Lord. *Amen.* (St. Paul's School).

81

HYMN: Little drops of water (*DS* 78; *SP* 365).

STORY LESSON: *Brand of Iceland* (page 203).

UNISON PRAYER:

The Prayer of Dedication

Jesus, Friend of the friendless; Helper of the poor; Healer of the sick;
Whose life was spent in doing good; Let us follow in Thy footsteps.
Make us strong to do right; Gentle with the weak; And kind to all who are in sorrow;
That we may be like Thee, our Lord and Master. *Amen.*

SILENT PRAYER:

Give to us, O Lord, the gift of courtesy, and let us never be too busy to be kind.

THE LORD'S PRAYER.

HYMN: Lord of all hopefulness, Lord of all joy (*DS* 79; *SP* 565).

CLOSING:

> Lord help me by Thy grace to be,
> Lowly and kind of heart like Thee;
> Gentle and loving, meek and mild,
> Thy servant, though a little child. *Amen.*
> (Isaac Watts).

SPRING   57   APRIL

JESUS ENTERS JERUSALEM
Preparation for Easter

OPENING:

Let us get ready for Easter by praising God that Jesus is alive and with us today.

Early one Sunday morning, the day after the Jewish Sabbath, Jesus set out on foot towards Jerusalem. He took the main path because many were with Him, but only He knew what was to come.

BIBLE READING: Jesus enters Jerusalem in triumph (Mark *11*. 1–10 *NEB*).

HYMN: Ride on! Ride on in majesty! (*DS* 58; *SP* 137).

PRAYER:

Lord Jesus, we remember this day when you rode into Jerusalem to face the danger that was there. Help us never to be afraid and give us the strength to go on in times of difficulty. As the children danced and sang in Jerusalem, may we praise Thee every day. *Amen.*

POETRY READING: *The Donkey* (page 141).

HYMN: The glory of our King was seen (*IP* 73).

STORY LESSON: *The Mark on the Donkey* (page 204).

PRAYER:

Almighty God, whose Son, our Saviour Jesus Christ was welcomed as a king by those who were soon to seek His death: Grant that we may never look for praise nor fear the blame of men, but to walk with strength and courage in the way that Thou art leading: through Jesus Christ our Lord. *Amen.*

SILENT PRAYER:

Let us be silent, and ask that we may be courageous—as Jesus was when He rode into Jerusalem to face His enemies.

THE LORD'S PRAYER.

HYMN: All glory, laud, and honour (*DS* 56; *SP* 135; *IP* 71).

CLOSING:

As on this day we keep the special memory of our Redeemer's entry into the city, so grant, O Lord, that now and ever He may triumph in our hearts. Let the King of grace and glory enter in, and let us give ourselves in praise before Him; through the same Jesus Christ our Lord. *Amen.* (Bishop Moule 1841, adapted).

SPRING	**58**	APRIL

HIS FRIENDS FORSAKE HIM

Preparation for Easter

OPENING:

Greater love hath no man than this, that a man lay down his life for his friends.

PRAYER:

Dear Heavenly Father, we are thinking this morning of Jesus, who gave His life that we might live. Fill our hearts with wonder and gladness for the great victory that has been won for us. *Amen.*

THEME:

When Jesus entered Jerusalem, the city was full of people. It was now Thursday, the day before the Passover, and in the evening Jesus and His friends sat down for the Passover Supper.

BIBLE READING: The Last Supper (Mat. *26*. 20–25 *NEB*).

HYMN: It is a thing most wonderful (*IP* 75).

READING:

After the Last Supper, Jesus went with His disciples to the garden of Gethsemane. He left His disciples to keep watch, while He went into the garden to pray, but they fell asleep and Jesus had to wake them.

BIBLE READING: The Arrest in the Garden (Mark *14*. 43–52 *NEB*).

HYMN: There is a green hill far away (*DS* 59; *SP* 131; *IP* 76).

STORY LESSON: *The Young Man in the White Sheet* (page 205).

84

Almighty God, we beseech thee graciously to behold this thy family, for which our Lord Jesus Christ was contented to be betrayed, and given up into the hands of wicked men, and to suffer death upon the cross, who now liveth and reigneth with Thee and the Holy Spirit, ever one God, world without end. *Amen.* (Ancient).

SILENT PRAYER:

Let us be quiet, as we think of the Easter story and all that it means to us.

THE LORD'S PRAYER.

HYMN: When I survey the wondrous cross (*DS* 60; *SP* 133).

CLOSING:

The God of hope fill you with all joy and peace in believing, that ye may abound in hope and in the power of the Holy Spirit. *Amen.*

SPRING 59 APRIL

EASTER FESTIVAL

THEME:

So we come to the most wonderful story of all. The Resurrection of our Lord on Easter morning. To all Christian people this is the keynote of our faith, that Jesus Christ, who died on the cross for our sins on Good Friday—rose again on Easter Day, and is alive for evermore.

PRAYER:

Dear Heavenly Father, we come to thank you this morning that Jesus is alive and with us today. Help us now to rejoice in the wonderful message of Easter Day. *Amen.*

FIRST READER:

> Ring out, you merry Easter bells,
> Ring out both loud and clear,
> And tell your joyful message,
> 'Rejoice, the Lord is near.'
> For happy Easter comes again,
> O hear the bells' sweet call,
> A comfort to all people,
> The gladdest day of all.

HYMN: Sing all ye Christian people! (*DS* 107; *SP* 163).

SECOND READER:

Early on the Sunday morning, while it was still dark, Mary of Magdala came to the tomb. She saw that the stone had been moved away from the entrance, and ran to Simon Peter and the other disciple, the one whom Jesus loved. 'They have taken the Lord out of his tomb,' she cried, 'and we do not know where they have laid him.' So Peter and the other set out and made their way to the tomb. They were running side by side, but the other disciple outran Peter and reached the tomb first. He peered in and saw the linen wrappings lying there, but did not enter. Then Simon Peter came up, following him, and he went into the tomb. He saw the linen wrappings lying, and the napkin which had been over his head, not lying with the wrappings but rolled together in a place by itself. Then the disciple who had reached the tomb first went in too, and he saw and believed; until then they had not understood the scriptures, which showed that he must rise from the dead. (John *20*. 1–9 *NEB*).

HYMN: The strife is o'er, the battle done (*DS* 64; *SP* 147).

THIRD READER:

[After the disciples had gone home] Mary stood at the tomb outside, weeping. As she wept, she peered into the tomb; and she saw two angels in white sitting there, one at the head, and one at the feet, where the body of Jesus had lain. They said to her, 'Why are you weeping?' She answered, 'They have taken my Lord away, and I do not know where they have laid him.' With these words she turned round and saw Jesus standing there, but did not recognize him. Jesus said to her, 'Why are you weeping? Who is it you are looking for?' Thinking it was the gardener, she said 'If it is you, sir, who removed him, tell me where you have laid him, and I will take him away.' Jesus said, 'Mary!' She turned to him and said, 'Rabbuni!' (which is Hebrew for 'My Master'). Jesus said, 'Do not cling to me, for I have not yet ascended to the Father. But go to my brothers, and tell them that I am now ascending to my Father and your Father, my God and your God.' Mary of Magdala went to the disciples with her news: 'I have seen the Lord!' she said, and gave them his message. (John *20*. 10–18 *NEB*).

HYMN: The head that once was crowned with thorns (*DS* 66; *SP* 175).

PRAYER:

We thank Thee, Lord Jesus, that springtime reminds us of the first Easter Day when Thou didst rise again to be with us always, and to bring us new life and joy every day. Give to us and all those we love the joy of Easter in our hearts and the living power of Thy Presence in our lives. For Thy Name's sake. *Amen.*

(R. E. Cleeve, CSSM).

SILENT PRAYER:

Jesus gave His Life for us. Let us think for a moment how we can live for Him.

THE LORD'S PRAYER.

HYMN: Come, ye children, sing to Jesus (*IP* 78).

CLOSING:

O ye who bear Christ's holy name,
Give God all praise and glory;
All ye who own his power, proclaim
Aloud the wondrous story!
The Love, the Wisdom, still adore
For ever and for evermore. *Amen.*

87

HEALTH AND STRENGTH

World Health Day, 7 April

THEME:

7 April is World Health Day, when we think of those who are sick and suffering all over the world. Today we remember that nations can join together to help the sick in all countries, and make them well again.

HYMN: Thine arm, O Lord, in days of old (*DS* 159; *SP* 287).

PRAYER:

We praise Thee, Heavenly Father, for the strength of
  our bodies and for life and health and movement,
      (*Together*) *We thank Thee, O God.*
For sturdy limbs and steady feet so that we can leap
  and run and play,
          We thank Thee, O God.
For hands to use to paint and draw and for the wonderful
  sense of touch,
          We thank Thee, O God.
For the quickness of mind and ear and eye to enjoy the
  gifts of the world that You have made,
          We thank Thee, O God.
For all these things we thank Thee, O God, today.
  May we remember those who are not so fortunate and to
  use our health and strength to make others glad. *Amen.*

HYMN: Hands to work and feet to run (*IP* 45).

BIBLE READING: Jesus heals many people (Mark *1.* 29–34 *NEB*).

STORY LESSON:

Today, doctors are working all over the world to cure and heal the sick. They have wonderful medicines and drugs and the knowledge of modern science but, long ago, people could not understand why there was sickness and disease. This is the story of how the Greeks thought that troubles came into the world:

Pandora's Box (page 206).

88

We thank you, Heavenly Father, for eyes that let us see
The clouds that cross the heavens, the leaf upon the tree;
We thank you, Heavenly Father, for ears that let us hear
The song of birds at daybreak and voices we hold dear;
We thank you, Heavenly Father, for strength to run and play,
Please help us to remember; these gifts are ours today.
Amen.

THE LORD'S PRAYER.

HYMN: Remember all the people (*DS* 140; *SP* 369).

CLOSING:

May God the Father of us all bless, direct, and keep us, and give us thankful hearts, now and for evermore. *Amen.*

SPRING   61   APRIL

OUR FRIENDS THE BIRDS
April Bird Song

OPENING:

Jesus said, 'Look at the birds of the air; they do not sow and reap and store in barns, yet your heavenly Father feeds them.'

THEME:

In April, the air is filled with the singing of birds. Let us thank God for them.

HYMN: All things bright and beautiful (*DS* 17; *SP* 444).

PRAYER:

O Lord Jesus, we remember that you have told us about God's care for the tiny sparrows and we thank you this morning for our friends the birds. May we help to look after them by giving them food and water and by treating them with kindness throughout the year. *Amen.*

POETRY READING: *Birds' Nests* (page 141).

STORY LESSON: *King of the Birds* (page 207).

PRAYER:

> Little bird on lightest wing,
> Who sings in every tree
> O listen while our praise we bring;
> God cares for you and me.
>
> Little bird 'tis sweet to see
> Our trust in God you share
> So may we praise Him merrily
> And thank Him for His care. *Amen.*

SILENT PRAYER:

'A tiny robin in a cage, puts all heaven in a rage.' Let us promise to be kind to all birds of the air.

THE LORD'S PRAYER.

HYMN: From out of a wood did a cuckoo fly (*DS* 3, Carols; *SP* 381).

READING:

> Said the robin to the sparrow,
> 'I should really like to know
> Why these busy human people,
> Seem to fret and worry so?'
> Said the sparrow to the robin,
> 'Friend, I think that it must be
> That they have no Heavenly Father
> Such as cares for you and me.'

CLOSING:

Jesus said, 'Are not sparrows five for twopence? And yet not one of them is overlooked by God. More than that, even the hairs of your head have all been counted. Have no fear; you are worth more than any number of sparrows.'

THE SKY ABOVE US

OPENING:

And God made two great lights; the greater light to rule the day, and the lesser light to rule the night; he made the stars also. . . and God saw that it was good. (Gen. *1*. 16–21 (selected).)

THEME:

Let us praise God for the wonders of the sky and the lights of heaven.

PRAYER:

O Father in heaven, we praise you for the wonderful lights that we can see in the sky above our heads; for the bright warm sun by day and the silvery moon and twinkling stars by night. As we see the wonders of light in the sky, may we remember that we are kept in the light of Thy love. *Amen.*

HYMN: Praise the Lord! Ye heavens adore him (*DS* 12; *SP* 624).

POETRY READING: *The Stars* (page 142).

HYMN: God who put the stars in space (*IP* 6).

STORY LESSON:

When looking at the night sky, people imagine that they can see pictures made by the stars. The Americans call one group of stars the Dipper (which is like a big ladle) and this, so they say, is how it got there:

The Legend of the Dipper (page 208).

PRAYER:

Praised be my Lord for all being,
And namely, praise for our Brother Sun.
Who bringeth us day, and light for seeing;
With joy he cometh his course to run.
Also for Sister Moon be praise,

And for the stars which stand on high;
Lovely and clear in heavenly ways,
Of Thee to us they do testify. *Amen.*

THE LORD'S PRAYER.

HYMN: Can you count the stars that brightly (*DS* 19; *SP* 462).

CLOSING:

The moon shines bright
And the stars give light
Before the break of day.
God bless you all,
Both great and small,
And send you a joyful day.

(Traditional)

SPRING 63 APRIL

APRIL SHOWERS
April Days

OPENING:

Praise ye the Lord:
For it is good to sing praises unto our God . . .
Who covereth the heaven with clouds,
Who prepareth rain for the earth,
Who maketh grass to grow upon the mountains.

(Psa. *147.* 1 and 8).

THEME:

The Bible says, 'He did good, and gave us rain from heaven.'
Let us thank God for the rain.

PRAYER:

Our Father in Heaven, we thank you for the gift of rain that
quenches the thirst of trees and flowers and makes rich harvests

grow. Help us to be happy indoors today and to remember that, without the rain, there would be no life on earth. *Amen.*

HYMN: Glad that I live am I (*DS* 114; *SP* 499).

PRAYER:

> For lovely flower and blossom gay,
> For trees and woods in bright array,
> For all the help the rain doth give
> To make all things to grow and live,
> We thank Thee, Lord, today. *Amen.*

HYMN: Down the air ev'rywhere (*Child Songs*, Carey Bonner).

STORY LESSON: *The Kind Raindrop* (page 209).

PRAYER:

Almighty God, we thank you for your promise to send the rains in their season, so that the land shall bear its crops and the trees their fruit and we may have plenty to eat. May we rejoice in the good that the rain does in all the world. *Amen.*

SILENT PRAYER:

God comes down in the rain, and the crop grows tall—This is the country faith, And best of all!

> (Norman Gale).

THE LORD'S PRAYER.

HYMN: We praise thee for the rain (2nd verse, *IP* 14).

CLOSING:

> God sends the sunshine and the rain
> To make us think, along the way,
> That life, with all its ups and downs,
> Is like a changing April day.
> It's easy to be happy, thro' all the sunny hours,
> But we must learn to smile and sing
> When sunshine turns to showers.

ST. MARK

St. Mark's Day, 25 April

OPENING:

Thus saith the Lord: Fear not: for I have redeemed thee, I have
called thee by thy name; . . . Fear not: for I am with thee.
(Isa. *43*. 1 and 5).

THEME:

In April is the special day for St. Mark, who wrote the second
book in the New Testament. Mark was the first one to write down
the story of Jesus.

PRAYER:

O Lord, our Heavenly Father, we think today of St. Mark who
wrote down for us the stories of Jesus. May we, like St. Mark, be
content to listen to the words of Jesus and to follow in the way of
our Lord and Master. *Amen.*

HYMN: For all the saints who from their labours rest (*DS* 97; *SP* 202).

BIBLE READING:

Here are some words of Jesus that appear only in St. Mark's
Gospel.

[Jesus] said, 'The kingdom of God is like this. A man scatters seed
on the land; he goes to bed at night and gets up in the morning,
and the seed sprouts and grows—how, he does not know. The
ground produces a crop by itself, first the blade, then the ear, then
full-grown corn in the ear; but as soon as the crop is ripe, he sets
to work with the sickle, because harvest-time has come.'
(Mark *4*. 26–29 *NEB*).

HYMN: God has given us a book full of stories (*IP* 20).

STORY LESSON: *Young John Mark* (page 210).

SILENT PRAYER:

Help us, O Lord, to be like young John Mark; to play the man and to meet all life's difficulties with courage.

UNISON PRAYER:

Be Thou with us every day,
In our work and in our play,
When we learn and when we pray.
Hear us, Holy Jesus.

Make us brave, without a fear,
Make us happy, full of cheer,
Sure that Thou art always near.
Hear us, Holy Jesus.

May we grow from day to day,
Glad to learn each holy way,
Ever ready to obey.
Hear us, Holy Jesus. *Amen.*

THE LORD'S PRAYER.

HYMN: Ye holy angels bright (*DS* 105; *SP* 701).

CLOSING:

The saint who first found grace to pen
The life which was the Life of Men
And shed abroad the Gospel's ray,
His fame we celebrate today.

And so may all whose minds are dark
Be led to truth by good St. Mark,
And after this our earthly strife,
Stand written in the Book of Life.
(Laurence Housman).

BEING HUMBLE

Baby Moles are Born

OPENING:

Jesus said, 'Come to me, all whose work is hard, whose load is heavy; and I will give you relief. Bend your necks to my yoke, and learn from me, for I am gentle and humble-hearted.'

(Mat. *11*. 28. *NEB*).

THEME:

Today we are thinking of being humble and letting someone else have the first place. Jesus Himself was not too proud to kneel down and wash the feet of His disciples.

BIBLE READING: Washing the disciple's feet (John *13*. 3–17 *NEB*).

HYMN: When I survey the wondrous cross (*DS* 60; *SP* 133).

PRAYER:

O Jesus Christ, who was not too proud to do the lowliest tasks, teach us today to be humble and let someone else have the first place. Make us kindly in thought, gentle in word, and helpful in deed, so that we may think always for the good of others and not for ourselves. We ask this for Thy Sake. *Amen.*

STORY LESSON: *A Husband for Miss Mole* (page 212).

PRAYER:

To God,
Whom no eye hath seen,
No ear hath heard
Yet who speaks to the heart
Of all that love Him:
To Him be praise and glory for ever and ever. *Amen.*

SILENT PRAYER:

Let us think in silence for a moment that, however humble the task, we will do it well.

96

THE LORD'S PRAYER.

HYMN: Sing a song of Maytime (*IP* 85).

CLOSING:

> He that is down need fear no fall,
> He that is low no pride;
> He that is humble ever shall
> Have God to be his Guide.
> (John Bunyan).

The grace of our Lord Jesus Christ, and the love of God, and the fellowship of the Holy Spirit, be with us all—now and always. *Amen.*

SUMMER   66   MAY

CLEANLINESS

OPENING:

> Who shall ascend into the hill of the Lord?
> Or who shall stand in his holy place?
> He that hath clean hands, and a pure heart.
> (Psa. *24*. 3).

THEME:

There is a saying that 'Cleanliness is next to Godliness'. Let us think how we can keep ourselves and everything around us clean and tidy.

PRAYER:

O Father God, we thank you for giving us bodies to take care of and to use for you. You have taught us that our bodies are the temples of the Holy Spirit. Help us to turn from bad things to good things and teach us how to keep ourselves fit and clean. *Amen.*

HYMN: In our work and in our play (*DS* 77; *SP* 538).

POETRY READING: *Mister Nobody* (page 142).

STORY LESSON: *The Pig Brother* (page 213).

PRAYER:

O God, give us clean thoughts, clean words, and clean hands.
Help us to stand for the hard right against the easy wrong.
Save us from habits that harm; teach us to work as hard and
play as fair in Thy sight alone as if all the world saw.
Forgive us when we are unkind, and help us to forgive them who
are unkind to us.
Keep us ready to help others at some cost to ourselves; send us
chances to do a little good every day, and to grow more like
our Lord Jesus Christ. *Amen.* (Wm. De Witt Hyde).

THE LORD'S PRAYER.

HYMN: Lord of health, thou life within us (*DS* 80; *SP* 567).

CLOSING:

Lord, teach us all that we should know;
In grace and wisdom may we grow;
The more we learn to do Thy will,
The better may we love Thee still. *Amen.*
(Isaac Watts).

SUMMER   67   MAY

RIGHT THINKING

THEME:

St. Paul once wrote these words: 'All that is true, all that is noble
all that is just and pure . . . fill all your thoughts with these things.
(*Phil. 4.* 8 *NEB*).

HYMN: Now in life's breezy morning (*DS* 82; *SP* 591).

PRAYER:

> God be in my head,
> And in my understanding;
> God be in mine eyes,
> And in my looking;
> God be in my mouth,
> And in my speaking;
> God be in my heart,
> And in my thinking;
> God be at mine end,
> And at my departing. *Amen.*

HYMN: I often think of God (*IP* 8).

STORY LESSON: *The Miller, the Son, and the Donkey* (page 214).

PRAYER:

> Give us, Heavenly Father, the will to think and do
>   always that which is right.
> Take our minds and think through them;
> Take our lips and speak through them;
> Take our lives that we may live as you would
>   have us live. *Amen.*

SILENT PRAYER:

Let us ask for God's help to think those thoughts that are honest and true.

THE LORD'S PRAYER.

HYMN: He who would valiant be (*DS* 74; *SP* 515).

CLOSING:

Grant to us, Lord, we beseech thee, the spirit to think and do always such things as be rightful; that we, who cannot do anything that is good without thee, may by thee be enabled to live according to thy will; through Jesus Christ our Lord. *Amen.*

(Leonine Sacramentary).

PRAYER

OPENING:

> O Thou, by whom we come to God,
> The Life, the Truth, the Way,
> The path of prayer Thyself hast trod,
> Lord, teach us how to pray. (REP).

THEME:

Today we are thinking about prayer. Jesus said: 'Whatever you pray for in faith you will receive.'

PRAYER:

O God, our Father, Thou has promised to hear Thy children when they pray to Thee. Help us now to pray, teach us what to ask for, help us to mean what we say, and give us grace to love Thee more, and to love the people for whom we pray; for Jesus Christ's sake. *Amen.* (*A Chain of Prayer*).

HYMN: Father, hear the prayer we offer (*DS* 123; *SP* 487).

POETRY READING: *God is so Good* (page 143).

HYMN: Gladly lift we hearts and voices (*IP* 19).

STORY LESSON: *The Prayer from Iona* (page 215).

PRAYER:

> Reach downward from Thy hidden throne
> And take my hands in prayer,
> And hold them, hold them in Thine own,
> In school and everywhere;
> And I will lift them up to Thee
> Quite often in the day;
> Do Thou each time take hold of me,
> That I may never stray. *Amen.* (Father Roche).

SILENT PRAYER:

Lord, give us faith when we pray, and make all our prayers unselfish.

100

One of the disciples said to Jesus: 'Lord, teach us to pray', and very simply Jesus taught them what we now call the Lord's Prayer.

THE LORD'S PRAYER.

HYMN: Jesus, good above all other (*DS* 125; *SP* 540).

CLOSING:

> He prayeth best who loveth best
> All things both great and small.
> For the dear Lord who loveth us,
> He made and loveth all.
>   (S. T. Coleridge).

SUMMER 69 MAY

CATHEDRALS AND GREAT CHURCHES
The Abbey Started, 16 May 1220

OPENING:

'I was glad when they said unto me, let us go into the house of the Lord.' (Psa. 122).

THEME:

On May 16 1220 they began to build the Abbey of Westminster. Today we are thinking of great cathedrals all over the world.

HYMN: City of God, how broad and far (*DS* 96; *SP* 468).

PRAYER:

O Lord, our Heavenly Father, we give Thee thanks for skilful craftsmen who had such faith in Thee that they built beautiful churches and great cathedrals in Thy Name and for Thy glory. *Amen.*

One day, a visitor was looking round St. Paul's Cathedral when it was only half finished. Going up to one of the masons he asked 'What are you doing?'

'Cutting stone,' replied the mason, without looking up.

'And you?' said the visitor to another workman, 'What are you doing?'

'Sawing wood,' replied a carpenter. Then the visitor found a humble labourer who was sweeping the floor.

'And what are you doing?' he asked.

The labourer looked up at the half finished building that was soaring above him. 'Sir,' he replied proudly, 'I am helping to build a cathedral.'

HYMN: Let all the world in every corner sing (*DS* 99; *SP* 556).

STORY LESSON: *The Abbey Church at West Minster* (page 216).

PRAYER:

> For the wonderful message of the great churches of
> the world,
> > (*Together*) *We give Thee thanks, O God.*
> For the work of masons who built lofty cathedrals of
> chiselled stone,
> > *We give Thee thanks, O God.*
> For the skill of artists and sculptors who painted and
> carved to make Thy church beautiful,
> > *We give Thee thanks, O God.*
> We praise Thee that throughout all ages, people have
> built in honour of Thy Name. *Amen.*

THE LORD'S PRAYER.

HYMN: Ye holy angels bright (*DS* 105; *SP* 701).

CLOSING:

Now unto the King eternal, immortal, invisible, the only wise God, be honour and glory for ever and ever. *Amen.*

COMMONWEALTH DAY
Commonwealth Day, 24 May

OPENING:

Make a joyful noise unto the Lord, all ye lands.
Serve the Lord with gladness, come before his presence
    with singing.
Know ye that the Lord he is God; it is he that hath
    made us, and not we ourselves. (Psa. *100*. 1–3).

THEME:

Today is Commonwealth Day when we think of the great brotherhood of nations that spreads over a quarter of the world.

PRAYER:

Dear Heavenly Father, we ask for Thy blessing upon people in
other lands, especially those who are hungry or ill. May we remember that we belong to the great brotherhood of nations and
help us all to live together in peace and goodwill. *Amen.*

HYMN: Remember all the people (*DS* 140; *SP* 369).

PRAYER:

Help us, Almighty Father, to see this world as Thou wouldst
have it be. Give us that wonderful gift of love so that we may
realise that all the world is our neighbour and be always ready to
help each other as Jesus Christ, Thy Son, taught by His example.
Amen.

STORY LESSON: *In the Beginning* (page 217).

PRAYER:

O Father God, may we remember that the children of other lands
are Thy children also. May the strong care for the weak, and
those who have give to those in need, so that we may all learn to
live with one another and so belong to Thy family, who has
taught us to pray . . .
    Our Father . . .

HYMN: All people that on earth do dwell (*DS* 1; *SP* 143).

CLOSING:

Through north and south and east and west
May God's immortal name be blest
Till everywhere beneath the sun
His Kingdom comes, His will be done. *Amen.*

SUMMER 71 MAY

ST. AUGUSTINE

St. Augustine's Day, 26 May

OPENING:

Father, we praise Thee, now the night is over. Active and
watchful, stand we all before Thee;
Singing we offer praise and meditation.
Thus we adore Thee. (St. Gregory).

THEME:

Today is the special day for St. Augustine, who brought
Christianity to England.

HYMN: Stand up, stand up for Jesus (*DS* 141; *SP* 646).

UNISON PRAYER:

God, our loving Father, hear us;
Bless us in our prayers today.
May we know that you are with us;
Keep us safe in every way.

All our lives your hand has led us
And we thank you for your care.
You have warmed and clothed and fed us;
Listen to our morning prayer.

May we learn to help each other;
Love and care for everyone.
Hear us, as we pray together,
As in Heaven, Thy will be done. *Amen.*

HYMN: I have a clear message from Jesus, my King (*IP* 48).

STORY LESSON: *The Fair Children of Angle Land* (page 218).

PRAYER:

O Father God, we thank you for your servants of old who spread the message of Jesus to all countries. Look down in mercy upon our native land and help us to help others wherever they may be. *Amen.*

THE LORD'S PRAYER.

HYMN: And did those feet in ancient time (*DS* 166; *SP* 446).

CLOSING PRAYER:

Lord Jesus Christ, Who alone art wisdom, Thou knowest what is best for us. Mercifully grant that it may happen to us only as it is pleasing to Thee and as it seems good in Thy sight this day; for Thy name's sake. *Amen.* (Henry VI, 1421).

SUMMER 72 MAY

WHITSUNTIDE

OPENING:

God is spirit and they that worship him must worship him in spirit and in truth.

THEME:

Whitsun is the birthday of the Church. The friends of Jesus, who knew and loved Him, were the first members of the Church and we remember this time when the Holy Spirit, the power of Jesus, came to them all, giving them strength to carry on His work on earth.

HYMN: O Holy Spirit, God (*DS* 89; *SP* 601).

PRAYER:

Our Father in Heaven, grant that the Holy Spirit may dwell within us; may His power make us strong; may His love make us gentle; may His truth make us free. *Amen.*

READER:

The name Whitsun comes from the words White Sunday because, long ago, people who had become Christians came to church dressed in white on that day.

HYMN: When God the Holy Spirit (*IP* 93).

READER:

The first Whitsun happened in Jerusalem at the Feast of Pentecost. The Jews were fond of these feasts or festivals, and fifty days after the Feast of the Passover they held the Feast of Pentecost (Pentecost means 'fifty'). Jews came from all parts, crowding into Jerusalem, and with them came people from foreign lands talking the strange languages from their own countries.

STORY LESSON: *The First Whitsuntide* (page 219).

PRAYER:

O Holy Spirit, help us to be like Jesus and help all Christian people to be like Him. Speak to us when we are tempted to do wrong, strengthen us to do right, and show us what we should do. *Amen.*

THE LORD'S PRAYER.

HYMN: Breathe on me, breath of God (*DS* 88; *SP* 458).

May God the Holy Spirit bless, preserve, and keep each one of us, now and for evermore. *Amen.*

SUMMER 73 JUNE

TRUST IN GOD
Trinity

OPENING:

For Thou art my hope, O Lord God;
Thou art my trust from my youth. (Psa. *71.* 5).

THEME:

In the Bible are these words 'Trust ye in the Lord for ever: For in the Lord Jehovah is everlasting strength.' (Isa. *26.* 4).

HYMN: O Praise ye the Lord! (*DS* 10; *SP* 351).

PRAYER:

O Lord, whose way is perfect, help us always to trust in Thy goodness. That walking with Thee and following Thee, we may always have quiet and contented minds, for Thou carest for us all. *Amen.*

POETRY READING: *The Country Faith* (page 143).

HYMN: Loving Father of all children (*IP* 27).

STORY LESSON: *Brothers of the Holy Trinity* (page 220).

PRAYER:

O Loving Father of us all,
Who by Thy power has set us free.
O may we answer to Thy call,

107

And evermore to trust in Thee.
There's nothing more we need to ask,
But faith to follow Thee until,
We've overcome and done the task
That's set, because it is Thy will. *Amen.*

SILENT PRAYER:

Let us ask, in silence, that we may so trust in God that no task is too difficult for us to do.

THE LORD'S PRAYER.

HYMN: Praise, my soul, the King of heaven (*DS* 25; *SP* 623).

CLOSING:

May this day be full of power that shall bring us nearer to Thee and make us more like Thee. May we so trust Thee this day, that when the day is over, our trust shall be firmer than ever. *Amen.*

SUMMER   74   JUNE

TREASURE

OPENING:

Jesus said, 'Where your treasure is, there will your heart be also.' (Mat. *6*. 21 *AV*).

THEME:

Today we are thinking of all the things that are precious to us, the things that are our treasures.

PRAYER:

A Litany for Good Things

For our own special belongings; our toys and games
and all the fun and laughter we enjoy together,
(*Together*) *We thank you, Heavenly Father.*

For our own pets and all tame animals that give us
so many happy hours,
We thank you, Heavenly Father.
For story books we like so much and pictures we look
at over and over again,
We thank you, Heavenly Father.
For the treasures of flowers in our gardens, fun by the
seaside and picnics in the country,
We thank you, Heavenly Father.
For all these treasures, we thank you, Heavenly Father.
Help us to use them and to share them whenever we can. *Amen.*

HYMN: To God who makes all lovely things (*IP* 13).

BIBLE READING: The treasure and the pearl (Mat. *13.* 44–46).

STORY LESSON:
Jesus told us that we think and worry too much about earthly
things instead of things that really matter. Here is a story about
a man who was greedy for riches.

The Forgotten Treasure (page 221).

PRAYER:
O God, the giver of all good gifts, we thank you for all the many
blessings that we have. Give us always contented minds, cheerful
hearts, and a generous spirit so that we may share your good gifts
with others. *Amen.*

THE LORD'S PRAYER.

HYMN: Praise him, praise him, all his children praise him!
(*DS* 119; *SP* 386 (V)).

CLOSING:
Around me when I look,
God's handiwork I see;
This world is like a picture book
To teach His name to me. *Amen.*
(J. E. Leeson).

GOD'S LOVE AND CARE

OPENING:

Enter into his gates with thanksgiving, and into his courts with praise: be thankful unto him, and bless his name. For the Lord is good. (Psa. *100*. 4–5).

HYMN: God who made the earth (*DS* 21; *SP* 358).

PRAYER:

A Child's Prayer

How wonderful is God's great love
That careth for a child like me,
And watches over me each hour,
So tenderly.

Oh, may Thy gracious Spirit, Lord,
Into my heart this day instil
The strength and courage joyfully,
To do Thy will. *Amen.*

(Amy Dark)

HYMN: Over the earth is a mat of green (*IP* 10).

PRAYER:

We thank Thee, Loving Father,
For all Thy tender care;
For food and clothes and shelter,
And all the world so fair. *Amen.*

(Anon.)

STORY LESSON: *Brittany Gold* (page 222).

PRAYER:

We give Thee thanks, O Lord our God, for Thy goodness at all times and in all places, because Thou hast shielded, rescued, helped and guided us all the days of our lives, and brought us unto this hour. Grant, in Thy goodness, that we may spend this day without

sin and in joyful reverence of Thee: through Jesus Christ our
Lord. *Amen.* (*Liturgy of St. Mark*—adapted).

SILENT PRAYER:
Let us be thankful for God's love and care, so that we may ever
look beyond the disappointments of today.

THE LORD'S PRAYER.

HYMN: Immortal, invisible, God only wise (*DS* 6; *SP* 535).

CLOSING:

I hear no voice, I feel no touch,
I see no glory bright;
But yet I know that God is near,
In darkness as in light.

He watches ever by my side,
And hears my whispered prayer;
The Father for His little child,
Both day and night doth care.

(Anon.)

SUMMER   76   JUNE

WORLD CHILDREN'S DAY

World Children's Day, 15 June

THEME:
15 June is called World Children's Day. On this day we think
especially of boys and girls all over the world and pray for their
health and happiness.

PRAYER:

O God, send Thy Spirit into men's hearts that they may hate war and love peace. Teach the children of every land that it is better to love one another than to fight, so that war may cease and Thy Kingdom of love and brotherhood may be set up through all the world, for the sake of Jesus Christ our Lord. *Amen.* (UNO.)

HYMN: Remember all the people (*DS* 140; *SP* 369).

BIBLE READING: Jesus calls the children (Mark *10.* 13–16 *NEB*).

HYMN: The clever papoose in the wigwam that lives (*IP* 12).

STORY LESSON: *The Children's Victory* (page 224).

PRAYER:

A Prayer for Children Overseas

O Father God, we ask Thy blessing upon children in other lands, especially those who are hungry and ill; those who are homeless and afraid; and those who do not know of Thy love.

May we remember that the children of all nations are Thy children; may the strong care for the weak and those who have, give to those who lack; may we learn to share with them and to provide for the sick and suffering; may we be to them the channels of Thy love, so shall we be members of Thy family, who has taught us to pray . . .   (UNO.)

Our Father . . .

THE LORD'S PRAYER.

HYMN: Children of the heavenly King (*DS* 68; *SP* 463).

CLOSING:

We bring to Thee our praises,
Receive them, Lord, we pray
And bless those other children
In countries far away.
Lord, grant that soon Thy light may shine,
Wide over all this world of Thine. *Amen.*
(REP.)

112

BEING FREE

Magna Carta, 15 June 1215

OPENING:

Jesus said, 'You shall know the truth, and the truth will set you free.' (John *8*. 32).

THEME:

Let us thank God that we are free to follow in His service.

PRAYER:

We give thee hearty thanks, O God, for the rest of the past night and for the gift of a new day with its opportunities of pleasing thee. Grant that we so pass its hours in the perfect freedom of thy service, that at eventide we may again give thanks unto thee; through Jesus Christ our Lord. *Amen.* (*Daybreak Office of the Eastern Church*).

HYMN: Hills of the North, rejoice (*DS* 137; *SP* 64).

PRAYER:

O Father God, you know that there are times when we long to be free to do as we like. Help us to do only those things which are honest and true and kind, and make us free to be the best that we can be. *Amen.*

HYMN: Sing a glad song to Christ the King (*IP* 38).

STORY LESSON: *King John and the Abbot of Canterbury* (page 225).

PRAYER:

Almighty God, whose service is perfect freedom; grant us so to follow the example of thy Son Jesus Christ, that we may find our joy in service, all the days of our lives. *Amen.*

SILENT PRAYER:

Let us be quiet for a moment and ask God that we may use our freedom in the service of others.

THE LORD'S PRAYER.

CLOSING:

Let us pray
That the Holy Spirit may dwell within us,
That His power may make us strong,
That His love may make us gentle,
That His truth may make us free. *Amen.*

SUMMER 78 JUNE

ST. ALBAN

St. Alban's Day, 22 June

OPENING:

Jesus said, 'Set your troubled hearts at rest. Trust in God always; trust also in me.' (John *14.* 1–2).

THEME:

Today is the special day for St. Alban who was one of the first Christians in Britain to stand up for Jesus, even to the end.

HYMN: Stand up, stand up for Jesus (*DS* 141; *SP* 646).
PRAYER:

Give us, O Lord, a steadfast will
To meet whatever there may be.
To face the future unafraid
With courage and serenity.
Give us, O Lord, a heart at peace
Our strength sustain, our faith increase. *Amen.*

HYMN: Jesus, hear our prayer (*IP* 50).

PRAYER:

May the Babe of Bethlehem be mine to tend;
May the Boy of Nazareth be mine for friend;

May the Man of Galilee my soul defend;
May the Christ of Calvary His courage lend;
Then, God, Thy holy angels send,
That I may see Thee at the end. *Amen.*
(Stephen Jack).

STORY LESSON: *The Saint of Holywell Hill* (page 226).

UNISON PRAYERS:

The Prayer of St. Ignatius of Loyola
Teach us, good Lord, to serve Thee as Thou deservest.
To give and not to count the cost.
To fight and not to heed the wounds.
To toil and not to seek for rest.
To labour and not to ask for any reward
Save that of knowing that we do Thy will. *Amen.*

THE LORD'S PRAYER.

HYMN: He who would valiant be (*DS* 74; *SP* 515).

CLOSING:

Lord, give us light upon our way
And wisdom for each passing day.
That we may live both straight and true
And do the best that we can do. *Amen.*

SUMMER   79   JUNE

SUMMER TIME

Midsummer Day, 24 June

OPENING:

The day is thine, the night also is thine.
Thou hast prepared the light and the sun,
Thou hast set all the borders of the earth;
Thou hast made summer and winter. (Psa. *74*. 16–17).

24 June is Midsummer Day and now is the time for the longest days of the year. Let us give thanks for the joys of summertime.

PRAYER:

A Litany for Summertime

For your gift of sunshine and the lovely long summer days,
(Together) We thank you, Heavenly Father.
For the fun of playing in the open air; for our games and
picnics and outings,
We thank you, Heavenly Father.
For the singing birds, the green trees and sweet-smelling
flowers,
We thank you, Heavenly Father.
For health and strength that make it possible for us to
enjoy the long days of summertime.
We thank you, Heavenly Father. Amen.

HYMN: Summer suns are glowing (*DS* 108; *SP* 7).

POETRY READING: *June Wind* (page 144).

HYMN: The sun shines down on the beautiful world (*IP* 86).

STORY LESSON:

In God's wonderful plan, the summer days are the longest of the year. This is how they thought it happened long, long ago.
Why Summer Days are Longer (page 227).

UNISON PRAYER:

God of Love and God of Light,
For Thy gift of sunshine bright,
For Thy care through day and night—
Our thanks to you, we bring.
Father as we older grow
Teach us day by day to know
All good gifts to Thee we owe—
Our thanks to you, we bring. *Amen.*
(Carey Bonner—adapted).

THE LORD'S PRAYER.

HYMN: Morning has broken (*DS* 147; *SP* 30).

CLOSING:

> God, our great Creator,
> Gave these summer days;
> May our hearts and voices
> Join to give Him praise. *Amen.*
>   (Anon.)

SUMMER   80   JUNE

ST. PETER

St. Peter's Day, 29 June

THEME:

Today is the special day when we think of Peter, the leader of the disciples. Peter was the brother of Andrew, who brought him to Jesus. 'And when Jesus saw him, He said, You are Simon, son of John. You shall be called Peter the Rock.'

PRAYER:

Dear God, hear our praises. We thank Thee for Jesus who showed men how to be strong and kind. We thank Thee for Peter, the leader of the apostles, who became strong to help those in trouble. Help us to be kind to everyone we meet and to do what we can to help them. *Amen.*

HYMN: For all the saints who from their labours rest (*DS* 97; *SP* 202).

BIBLE READING: Feed my sheep (John *21*. 9–17 *NEB*).

PRAYER:

> Jesus Gentle Shepherd,
> Whose love will never sleep;
> Guard us, if we ever wander

117

From Thy flock, like foolish sheep.
In Thy love do Thou enfold us,
Guide and lead us every day;
Like a lamb upon your shoulder
Bring us back if we should stray. *Amen.*

HYMN: Loving Shepherd of thy sheep (*IP* 28).

STORY LESSON: *Peter and John at the Beautiful Gate* (page 228).

PRAYER:

Lord Jesus, who didst send out Thy disciples to spread the Gospel in all the world, we thank Thee for Thy apostle St. Peter. We would ask Thee to strengthen all those who, today, are spreading the Good News to other lands and grant that the day may soon come when all the earth is full of the knowledge of God. *Amen.*

THE LORD'S PRAYER.

HYMN: Far round the world thy children sing their song
(*DS* 135; *SP* 299).

CLOSING:

[May we] grow in grace, and in the knowledge of our Lord and Saviour, Jesus Christ. To him be glory both now and for ever. *Amen.* (2 Peter *3. 18 AV*).

SUMMER 81 JULY

THE COUNTRYSIDE
Summer Days

OPENING:

Jesus said, 'Consider the lilies of the field, how they grow; they toil not, neither do they spin: And yet I say unto you, That even Solomon in all his glory was not arrayed like one of these.'
(Mat. *6. 28–29 AV.*)

118

In summertime, the countryside is ablaze with colour. Let us praise God, today, for the woods and the fields, for parks and open spaces.

PRAYER:
O God, who hast made all things beautiful, give us a love of the countryside, its lanes and meadows, its woods and streams and clean, open spaces; and let us keep it fresh and unspoilt for those who shall come after us. *Amen.*

HYMN: God who made the earth (*DS* 21; *SP* 358).

POETRY READING: *God's Providence* (page 144).

PRAYER:
Father, we thank Thee for all Thy gifts;
For the life-giving sun and the life-giving rain,
For the woods and fields,
For the flowers and birds,
For the rivers and the sea,
For the hills and valleys, and for the glory of the open sky.
For eyes to see, and health to enjoy
Everything around us rejoices.
Make us also to rejoice, and give us thankful hearts. *Amen.*

HYMN: Over the earth is a mat of green (*IP* 10).

STORY LESSON: *A Little Drop of Water* (page 229).

PRAYER:
We thank our loving Father God,
Who gives us everything.
Who sends the sunshine and the showers,
And makes rich harvests spring.
He clothes the lilies of the field
And feeds each bird and beast;
And all may share His tender care
The greatest and the least. *Amen.*
(Carey Bonner).

SILENT PRAYER:
With our eyes closed, let us think of a place in the country that we like—and thank God for it.

HYMN: Little drops of water (*DS* 78; *SP* 365).

CLOSING:

> The air we breathe, the sky, the breeze,
> The light without us and within,
> Life with its unlocked treasuries,
> God's riches are for all to win. *Amen.*

SUMMER   82   JULY

COLOURS

Nature in July

OPENING:

The glory of the Lord shall endure for ever,
The Lord shall rejoice in his works. (Psa. *104. 31*).

THEME:

Today we are thinking about colours. How dull the world would be without God's gift of all the colours that there are!

PRAYER:

> *A Litany for Colour*
>
> For the blue of the sky and gold of sunlight,
> > (*Together*) *Dear Father God, we thank you.*
> For the green and brown of trees and the many coloured leaves,
> > *Dear Father God, we thank you.*
> For all the differing pinks and mauves and crimson of summer flowers,
> > *Dear Father God, we thank you.*
> For the white of snow and clouds and for all the colours of the rainbow,
> > *Dear Father God, we thank you.*

For all the brightness of colours that we enjoy from
day to day.
Dear Father God, we thank you. Amen.

HYMN: All things bright and beautiful (*DS* 17; *SP* 444).

POETRY READING: *Yellow* (page 144).

PRAYER:
> O God, who has given us eyes to see
> The colours, that are here and there.
> Give us a heart to find out Thee
> And see your Presence everywhere. *Amen.*

STORY LESSON: *The Creeper that turns Crimson* (page 230).

PRAYER:
> Sky so bright
> Blue and light
> Stars how many hast thou?
>> Countless stars.
> Countless times
> Shall our God be praised now.
> Forest green
> Cool, serene,
> Leaves how many hast thou?
>> Countless leaves
> Countless times
> Shall our God be praised now. *Amen.*

SILENT PRAYER:
Let us keep our eyes closed and imagine what the world would
be like without God's gift of colours.

THE LORD'S PRAYER.

HYMN: Daisies are our silver (*DS* 112; *SP* 354).

CLOSING:
> The lilies so white,
>> And the bluebells so blue
> The buttercups bright
>> And the sweet daisies too,

Are sent by the Father
As gifts from above.
And bring us this message
That God's name is love. *Amen.*

GOD'S TINY CREATURES
Nature in July

THEME:

This is the time of the year when butterflies and ladybirds may be seen, the song of the grasshopper is heard and the first glow-worms show their silvery light. Let us praise God for all tiny creatures.

HYMN: I love God's tiny creatures (*DS* 22; *SP* 361).

PRAYER:

All things which live below the sky,
Or move within the sea,
Are creatures of the Lord most high,
And brothers unto me.

Almighty Father, King of Kings,
The lover of the meek,
Make me a friend of helpless things,
Defender of the weak. *Amen.*
(E. J. Brailsford).

POETRY READING: *The Butterfly* (page 145).

HYMN: O Father, the maker of beautiful things (*IP* 9).

STORY LESSON: *The First Butterflies* (page 231).

PRAYER:

O Father God, open our eyes to see you everywhere, even in the tiniest creatures that you have put on earth to do your work.
The coral-coated ladybird,
The velvet humming bee,
The brightly painted butterfly,
All creatures speak of Thee. *Amen.*

THE LORD'S PRAYER.

HYMN: For the beauty of the earth (*DS* 113; *SP* 494).

CLOSING:

Jesus divine,
Dear Brother mine
Be with me all the day.
And when the light
Has turned to night
Be with me still I pray.
Where'er I be,
Come Thou with me,
And never go away. *Amen.*

(W. Roche).

SUMMER   84   JULY

THE FARM

Thoughts of Holidays

OPENING:

He causeth the grass to grow for the cattle, and herb for the service of man. That he may bring forth food out of the earth. (Psa. *104.* 14).

What a wonderful place a farm is! With its fields and orchards, stables and barns, the animals and the busy people who work there. Let us make a prayer to God for all these things.

PRAYER:

Great Father in Heaven, we thank you for the good earth and
for all things that grow in the field and orchard.
For the farmers and busy people who work that we may eat;
For the shepherds and herdsmen who care for sheep and cattle;
For those who cut the hedgerows and plant the woods;
For the horses and all animals that live on the farm;
For tractors and machinery that lighten the work;
For all these things, we thank you. *Amen.*

HYMN: Let us, with a gladsome mind (*DS* 110; *SP* 12).

POETRY READING: *Down on the Farm* (page 145).

HYMN: O Father, the maker of beautiful things (*IP* 9).

STORY LESSON: *When Jesus was Thirsty* (page 232).

PRAYER:

O God, great and wonderful, who hast created the heavens, dwelling in the light and beauty thereof; Who hast made the earth, revealing Thyself in every flower that opens; let not mine eyes be blind to Thee, neither let my heart be dead, but teach me to praise Thee even as the lark which offereth her song at daybreak. *Amen.*

(Prayer of St. Isidore).

THE LORD'S PRAYER.

HYMN: We thank you, Lord of Heaven (*DS* 116; *SP* 692).

CLOSING:

Hear us, O Lord,
Make clean our hearts
And teach our hands the skill
Our minds the thoughts to use for Thee,
That we may do Thy will. *Amen.*

THE TREES

Thoughts of Holidays

OPENING:

Out of the ground made the Lord God to grow every tree that is pleasant to the sight and good for food. (Gen. *2. 9*).

THEME:

Today we are thinking of trees, their beauty and strength and the life they give to the countryside. Man has made many things, but only God can make a tree.

PRAYER:

Teach us, Father, how to be
Kind and patient as a tree.
A tree that looks to you all day
And lifts her leafy arms to pray;
And may the prayer that trees impart
Find an answer in our hearts
So that our lives may always be
A prayer of worship unto Thee. *Amen.*

HYMN: We thank thee, Lord, for this fair earth (*DS* 115; *SP* 691).

POETRY READING: *The Song of the Trees* (page 145).

HYMN: For the beauty of the earth (*IP* 4).

STORY LESSON: *The Angel of the Trees* (page 233).

PRAYER:

As the trees under the open sky give us, O Lord, the strength and patience to be upright wherever we may be. As the wind stirs the trees into song so may our own lives be made a melody unto Thee, for Jesus Christ's sake. *Amen.*

THE LORD'S PRAYER.

CLOSING:

Now unto God the Creator, eternal, immortal, invisible, the only wise God, be honour and glory for ever and ever. *Amen.*

SUMMER 86 JULY

THE SEASIDE

Thoughts of Holidays

OPENING:

The sea is his, and he made it; and his hands formed the dry land. (Psa. *95. 5*).

THEME:

Soon many of you will be going to the seaside for the holiday, to enjoy the sand and the sea. Here is a poem about a sea-shell.

POETRY READING: *The Sea-shell* (page 146).

PRAYER:

We thank you, Heavenly Father, for all the joys of the
        seaside.
For the soft golden sands and the waves breaking upon
    the shore:
For high cliffs and deep caves, the beauty of shells
    and the treasures found in rocky pools.
For the fun of paddling and building sand-castles and
        for health and strength gained by the sea,
            We thank you, Heavenly Father. *Amen.*

HYMN: Little drops of water (*DS* 78; *SP* 365).

STORY LESSON: *Jesus by the Seaside* (page 234).

O God, we thank Thee for the salt sea and the running tide, for the everlasting hills, for the trees and for the grass under our feet. Grant us, we pray Thee, a heart wide open for all this joy and beauty so that we do not pass by with unseeing eyes when even a grain of sand has a place in Thy Universe. *Amen.*

SILENT PRAYER:

Let us think, in silence, of the greatness of the seas and of the mighty oceans that span the world.

THE LORD'S PRAYER.

HYMN: All things which live below the sky (*DS* 18; *SP* 445).

CLOSING:

> God of Life and God of Love,
> We read Thee in the sky above;
> We read Thee in the earth below,
> In seas that swell and streams that flow.
> We read Thee in the flowers, the trees,
> The freshness of the fragrant breeze.
> The songs of birds upon the wing,
> The joy of summer and of spring. *Amen.*
> (H. Bonnar, *Songs of Praise*).

SUMMER   87   JULY

SPORTS AND GAMES
Sports Day

OPENING:

St. Paul once wrote: 'You know that at the sports all the runners run the race, though only one wins the prize. Like them, run to win!' (1 Cor. *9.* 24).

O Lord Jesus, who played with boys and girls in Galilee, be with us today in our sports and games. Help us to play fairly; to be generous when we win and cheerful when we lose. Teach us to value the game for its own sake and not for any prize to be won; and so may courage abound with cheerfulness, for Thy Name's sake. *Amen.*

HYMN: Lord of health, thou life within us (*DS* 80; *SP* 567).

PRAYER:

> Holy God, who madest me
> And all things else to worship Thee;
> Keep me fit in mind and heart,
> Body and soul to take my part.
> Fit to stand, fit to run,
> Fit for sorrow, fit for fun.
> Fit for work and fit to play,
> Fit to face life day by day:
> Holy God, who madest me,
> Make me fit to worship Thee. *Amen.*
>   (W. B. White, *Prayers in Poetry*).

STORY LESSON: *The Golden Apples* (page 235).

UNISON PRAYER:

> *The Prayer of St. Ignatius of Loyola*

Teach us, good Lord, to serve Thee as Thou deservest.
To give and not to count the cost.
To fight and not to heed the wounds.
To toil and not to seek for rest.
To labour and not to ask for any reward
Save that of knowing that we do Thy will. *Amen.*

THE LORD'S PRAYER.

HYMN: In our work and in our play (*DS* 77; *SP* 538).

CLOSING:

May the grace of courage, gaiety, and the quiet mind fill our hearts this day and always. *Amen.*

END OF TERM

St. Christopher's Day, 25 July

OPENING:

Enter into his gates with thanksgiving, And into his courts with praise . . . For the Lord is good; his mercy is everlasting, And his truth endureth to all generations. (Psa. *100*. 4–5).

THEME:

This is the last day of term and the end of the school year. Let us thank God for all we have learned and enjoyed at school.

PRAYER:

O Lord, our Heavenly Father, we give Thee humble and hearty thanks for the blessings we have received throughout this year; for health and strength, for progress made, and for the joys of friendship. We ask for Thy blessing on our holidays and grant that as we go our different ways, we shall speak and think and act as true followers of Thy Son, Jesus Christ, our Lord. *Amen.*

HYMN: The Lord's my Shepherd (*DS* 214) (Crimond).

PRAYER:

Direct us, O Lord, in all our doings and further us with Thy continual help, that in all our works begun, continued, and ended in Thee, we may glorify Thy Holy Name for ever. *Amen.*

STORY LESSON:

The end of term is a milestone in the lives of most of us in school. Many will be travelling in different directions, so let us hear again the story of St. Christopher, the patron saint of travellers, whose special day is 25 July.

The Legend of St. Christopher (page 236).

129

The Prayer of Dedication

Jesus, Friend of the friendless; Helper of the poor; Healer of the sick;
Whose life was spent in doing good; Let us follow in Thy footsteps.
Make us strong to do right; Gentle with the weak; And kind to all who are in sorrow;
That we may be like Thee, our Lord and Master. *Amen.*

SILENT PRAYER:

Let us ask for God's blessing on our homes and holidays, and make a promise to be more thoughtful in the days to come.

THE LORD'S PRAYER.

HYMN: God be with you till we meet again (*DS* 164; *SP* 334).

CLOSING:

The Lord bless you and keep you,
The Lord make his face to shine upon you and be gracious unto you,
The Lord lift up the light of his countenance upon you and give you peace, now and for evermore. *Amen.*

POETRY READINGS

Come, Follow Me!

As Jesus walked in Galilee
Down by the shores of that blue sea,
Among His friends the fishermen
Simon, Andrew, James and John.
    They heard the call, 'Come, follow Me!'
    And in His steps went joyfully.

As in the Master's steps they trod,
They followed then the Son of God,
His voice was heard by Philip too,
And by his friend Bartholomew.
    All heard the call, 'Come, follow Me!'
    And in His steps went joyfully.

The steps of Jesus then were bent
And by the seat of custom went,
To Matthew counting out his gold
No longer Levi as of old.
    To heed His call, 'Come, follow Me!'
    Left all to follow joyfully.

To north and south and east and west,
Throughout the world His Name be blessed.
To follow Him in every way
And listen for His voice today.
    To hear the call, 'Come, follow Me!'
    And in His steps go joyfully.

Out in the Fields with God

The little cares that fretted me
I lost them yesterday,
Among the fields above the sea,
Among the winds at play.

Among the lowing of the herds,
The rustling of the trees,
Among the singing of the birds,
The humming of the bees.

The foolish fears of what might happen,
I cast them all away
Among the clover-scented grass
Among the new-mown hay
Among the husking of the corn,
Where drowsy poppies nod,
Where ill thoughts die and good are born—
Out in the fields with God.

(ANONYMOUS).

Autumn Leaves

The trees look so lovely
Their leaves have all turned
To yellow and crimson and brown.
It looks just as though
They were all set on fire
Before they came fluttering down.
Wherever I step
They rustle along
And crackle beneath my tread,
And I scuffle my feet
Through a glorious glow
Of yellow, and orange, and red

(M. G. HASKINS).

Kindness to Animals

Little children, never give
Pain to things that feel and live;
Let the gentle robin come
For the crumbs you save at home—
As his meat you throw along
He'll repay you with a song;
Never hurt the timid hare
Peeping from her green grass lair,
Let her come and sport and play
On the lawn at close of day;

The little lark goes soaring high
To the brightness of the sky,
Singing as if 'twere always spring,
And fluttering on beating wing,—
Oh! Let him sing his happy song,
Nor do these gentle creatures wrong.

Story Books

I like to look at a story book
And read the tales of long ago,
Of princes, kings, and fairy queens,
And witches, too, I like to know.

There's magic caves and forty thieves,
Aladdin and the Sandman, too,
Cinderella and her slipper,
Hunting horn and Boy in Blue.

But I must learn to treat with care
The stories through the ages
And never throw a book about,
Or tear the lovely pages.

Every Day

There are so many things to do today
    In city, field, and street,
And people are going everywhere,
    With quickly hurrying feet.

Some are ploughing and sowing the seed,
    And some are reaping the grain;
And some, who worked the whole night through,
    Are coming home again.

Over the hills the shepherd goes,
    While in the busy town
People and carts and motor cars
    Are running up and down;

And everywhere they come and go
In sun and rain and sleet,
That we may have warm clothes to wear,
And food enough to eat.

(MARY OSBORN).

The Fairy Flute

My brother has a little flute
Of gold and ivory.
He found it on a summer night
Within a hollow tree,
He plays it every morning
And every afternoon,
And all the little singing-birds
Listen to the tune.
He plays it in the meadows,
And everywhere he walks
The flowers start a-nodding
And dancing on their stalks.
He plays it in the village,
And all along the street
The people stop to listen,
The music is so sweet.
And none but he can play it
And none can understand,
Because it is a fairy flute
And comes from Fairyland.

(ROSE FYLEMAN).

What was it Like?

What was it like on Christmas morn—
The day when Mary's Babe was born?

Was it dull—or was it fine?
I wonder, did the bright sun shine?

Did the wind howl loud and grand
While Mary held her small Babe's hand?

Or was it still and calm and fair
When shepherds came to kneel in prayer?

134

Perhaps it snowed without a sound
As Wise Men's gifts lay on the ground.

I often wonder, on Christmas morn,
What was it like When Christ was born.

(W. O'NEILL).

The Little Fir Tree

At Christmas time so long ago,
The winds were blowing high and low;
A little green fir tree grew by the Inn,
A little fir tree straight and slim.

And, looking up, across the night
The fir tree saw the Star so bright.
The little fir tree wondered why
The Star was moving in the sky.

The star shone over Bethlehem
Over the stable inn, and then
The little green fir tree shone with light,
Lit by the star that wintry night.

(MARGARET ROSE).

Christmastide

Snow time, sad time,
        The world is growing old;
The shadows fall across the wall,
        The night is wan and cold;
When lo! the joyous songs arise
Of angels in the starry skies.

Child time, glad time,
        The world is young again;
The starlight streams, the holly gleams
        Upon the frosted pane,
Grant us, dear Lord, a place beside
The baby Christ, at Christmastide!

(WILLIS BOYD ALLEN).

The Shepherds Slept

The shepherds slept; and, glimmering faint,
    With twist of thin, blue smoke,
Only their fires crackling flames
    The tender silence broke—
Save when a young lamb raised his head,
    Or, when the night wind blew,
A nesting bird would softly stir,
    Where dusky olives grew—

And all their gentle sleepy flock
    Looked up, then slept again,
Nor knew the light that dimmed the stars
    Brought endless peace to men—
Nor even heard the gracious words
    That down the ages ring—
'The Christ is born! the Lord has come,
    Good will on earth to bring.'

Then o'er the moonlit, misty fields,
    Dumb with the world's great joy,
The shepherds sought the white-walled town,
    Where lay the baby boy—
And oh, the gladness of the world,
    The glory of the skies,
Because the longed-for Christ looked up,
    In Mary's happy eyes!
            (MARGARET DELAND (adapted)).

The Three Kings

There came three kings from Eastern land
Started by God's Almighty Hand,
To Christward through Jerusalem
Unto the Crib at Bethlehem.
    God thither, too, our footsteps guide
    To serve that Babe at every tide.

Why, Herod, honour so the kings,
Their minds are set on other things.
Forth from the stately court in speed
They to the lowly crib proceed.
    God, may we never swerve aside
    But keep Thy path, what'er betide.

No sooner come within the stall
Then down upon the knee they fall,
And offer Him, in order meet
Gold, myrrh, and incense passing sweet.
God, take our gifts both great and small
Heart, soul, life, limb, name, substance—all.
(*The Cowley Carol Book*).

Come Away to Bethlehem

Come away to Bethlehem
On a Christmas Day
Bring the Christ Child ringing bells
To make His cradle gay;
You've a shining apple
And I've a silver star
To greet Him on His birthday
We have travelled far.

Come away to Bethlehem
(The trees are all in white);
To find the little Jesus
We shall need no light,
For above His stable
Burns the star so clear,
So knock softly on the door
And say that we are here.

The Magi came with costly gifts
Across the silent snows,
But we have only little things
To give the World's Rose;
You've a shining apple
And I've a silver star
To greet Him on His birthday
We have travelled far.
(JOYCE WINBOLT).

What will the New Year Bring?

What will the New Year bring?
In wintertime a touch of snow
To make our ears and fingers glow,

137

And sparkling frost at early dawn
With robin redbreast on the lawn.
What will the New Year bring?
Snowdrops in spring will raise their heads
In forest glades and garden beds.
Come summer, when the woods are green,
Among the flowers the bees are seen
And golden sands down by the sea
Where waves come splashing merrily.
What will the New Year bring?
At harvest time the golden grain
To stack into the sheaves again
With apples red and acorns brown
As yellow leaves come tumbling down.
What will the New Year bring?
God's gifts for everything.

White World

Snow was falling in the night
We were fast asleep;
Now the world is cold and white—
Snow is soft and deep.

See the frosty pattern drawn
On the window pane,
Curly leaf and graceful fern,
Soon to melt again.

As the snow comes softly down,
See each tiny flake:
Every one a perfect star,
As only God can make.

(ROSE NETTLETON).

Four Things

Four things a man must learn to do
If he would make his record true;
To think without confusion clearly,
To love his fellow men sincerely;
To act from honest motives purely;
To trust in God and Heaven securely.

(HENRY VAN DYKE).

The Voice of God

I bent unto the ground
And I heard the quiet sound
Which the grasses make when they
Come up laughing from the clay

'We are the voice of God', they said
Thereupon I bent my head
Down again that I might see
If they truly spoke to me.

But around me everywhere
Grass and tree and mountain were
Thundering in a mighty glee,
'We are the voice of deity'.

And I leapt from where I lay,
I danced upon the laughing clay,
And to the rock that sang beside,
'We are the voice of God', I cried.

(JAMES STEPHENS).

Just for Jesus

Jesus, I kneel down to say
Thank you for another day.

For hands to feel and eyes to see
And all your loving gifts to me.

Teach me in your words to talk
Help me in your ways to walk.

Guide and bless me from above,
Jesus, it is you I love!

(LYSBETH BOYD BORIE).

The Wind

I saw you toss the kites on high
And blow the birds about the sky;
And all around I heard you pass,
Like dancing feet across the grass—
    O wind, a-blowing all day long,
    O wind, that sings so loud a song!

I saw the different things you did,
But always you yourself you hid,
I felt you push, I heard you call,
I could not see yourself at all—
    O wind, a-blowing all day long,
    O wind, that sings so loud a song!

O you that are so strong and cold,
O blower, are you young or old?
Are you a beast of field and tree,
Or just a stronger child than me?
    O wind, a-blowing all day long,
    O wind, that sings so loud a song!
              (R. L. STEVENSON).

Mother's Hands

The first hands that I ever knew
Once saved me from a fall.
They marked my growing height each year
Upon the kitchen wall.

They taught me how to hold a pen
When I would write a letter,
When I was ill, they'd comfort me,
And help to make me better.

They do such kind and useful things
For me and many others;
I hope that when I'm big, my hands
May be just like my mother's.
              (ROSE NETTLETON).

Spring

Spring is a maiden, dressed in green,
The youngest, fairest, ever seen!
Her skin is soft, and snowdrop white,
And fresh as any dewdrop bright.
Her eyes are shining violet-blue,
Her flowing hair, of primrose hue,
Has caught the pale gold spring sunbeams
In a silken trap, from which it seems

140

They do not want to leave at all!
Her mouth is a budding-blossom small,
Where'er she walks, the spring flowers grow,
And soft spring breezes start to blow!

(P. M. BOLGER).

The Donkey

When fishes flew and forests walked
　　And figs grew upon thorn,
Some moment when the moon was blood,
　　Then surely I was born;

With monstrous head and sickening cry
　　And ears like errant wings,
The devil's walking parody
　　On all four-footed things.

The tattered outlaw of the earth,
　　Of ancient crooked will;
Starve, scourge, deride me: I am dumb,
　　I keep my secret still.

Fools! For I also had my hour;
　　One far fierce hour and sweet:
There was a shout about my ears,
　　And palms before my feet!

(G. K. CHESTERTON).

Birds' Nests

The skylark's nest among the grass
　　And waving corn is found;
The robin's on a shady bank,
　　With oak leaves strewn around.

The wren builds in an ivied thorn,
　　Or old and ruined wall;
The mossy nest, so covered in,
　　You scarce can see at all.

The cuckoo makes no nest at all
　　But through the wood she strays
Until she finds one snug and warm,
　　And there her eggs she lays.

141

Rooks build together in a wood,
    And often disagree;
The owl will build inside a barn
    Or in a hollow tree.

The habits of each little bird,
    And all its patient skill,
Are surely taught by God Himself
    And ordered by His Will.

The Stars

What do the stars do
    Up in the sky,
Higher than the wind can blow
    Or the clouds fly?

Each star in its own glory
    Circles, circles still;
As it was lit to shine and set
    And do its Master's will.
                    (CHRISTINA ROSETTI).

Mister Nobody

I know a funny little man,
    As quiet as a mouse,
Who does the mischief that is done
    In everybody's house!
There's no one ever sees his face,
    And yet we all agree
That every plate we break was cracked
    By Mister Nobody.

'Tis he who always tears our books,
    Who leaves the doors ajar,
He pulls the buttons from our clothes,
    And scatters pins afar;
That squeaky door will always squeak,
    Because of this, you see—
We leave the oiling to be done
    By Mister Nobody.

142

The finger-marks upon the door
    By none of *us* are made;
We never leave the blinds undrawn
    To let the curtains fade;
The ink we never spill; the boots
    That lying round you see
Are not *our* boots; they all belong
    To Mister Nobody.
                    (ANONYMOUS).

God is so Good

God is so good that He will hear,
    Whenever children humbly pray;
He always lends a gracious ear
    To what the youngest child may say.

His own most holy Book declares
    He loves good little children still,
And that he listens to their prayers,
    Just as a tender father will.
                    (JANE TAYLOR).

The Country Faith

Here in the country's heart
Where the grass is green,
Life is the same sweet life
As it e'er hath been.

Trust in a God still lives,
And the bell at morn
Floats with a thought of God
O'er the rising corn.

God comes down in the rain,
And the crop grows tall—
This is the country faith,
And best of all.
                    (NORMAN GALE).

143

June Wind

How softly does the warm wind blow!
It scatters all the hawthorn snow,
While chestnut-bloom bestrews the grass
To tell that spring days swiftly pass.

How softly does the warm wind sing!
And soon, I know that it will bring
The woodbine's scent, the rose's, too,
To tell that summer's here anew.

(MALCOLM HEMPHREY).

God's Providence

God gives so many lovely things!
He gives the bird its feathery wings,
The butterfly its colours fair,
The bee a velvet coat to wear.

He gives the garden all its flowers,
And sun to make them grow, and showers;
Red apples for the old bent tree,
Wheat in the meadow blowing free;

Cool grass upon the summer hills,
And silvery streams to turn the mills.
He gives the shining day, and then
The quiet, starry night again.

(NANCY BYRD TURNER).

Yellow

I like a colour that's bright and gay,
A yellow 'mac' for a rainy day.

And buttercups on a field of green
And fairy gold for a Fairy Queen.

I like the gold of the morning sun,
Coming to tell me day has begun.

And shining softly through the night,
The yellow glow of the candle-light.
(HELEN L. BLACK).

The Butterfly

I know a little butterfly
With tiny golden wings;
He plays among the summer flowers
And up and down he swings.
He sparkles in the shining sun
With yellow, blue and gold,
And when he settles on a stone
He's glorious to behold;
For just a moment in the day
He really has the power
To turn that brown and mossy stone
Into a summer flower.
(A. G. P.)

Down on the Farm

Down on the farm, now summer's come,
The reapers work and the tractors hum.
Cows go wandering down the lane
Back to the cool, green grass again.
The chickens cluck and the cockerels crow
As into the pond the white ducks go.
With horses big and lambs so small
It is such fun to see them all
And for all these things we say
Thank you, Father God, today.

The Song of the Trees

There sounds a voice where trees rejoice
    In wood and lane and dell;
In ev'ry place God's love and grace
    The whispering branches tell.

The mighty oaks that guard the glade
    Declare to all the story
Of Him who hath the oak trees made,
    In all their strength and glory.

145

The pines that live, though days grow chill
        And earth its snow-wreath wearing,
Remind us that our Father still
        In sun or shine, is caring.
                    (M. SCOTT HAYCRAFT).

The Sea-shell

I have a sea-shell from the seas
Where the great fishes swim,
With golden scales
And silver tails,
Through waters green and dim.

I held my sea-shell to my ear
And heard the long winds blow,
Now singing of the ocean's bed,
Of coral forests, flame and red,
And branches white as snow.

I have a shell from far away;—
A diver brought it me,
And when I listen I can hear,
Like trumpets blown, now faint, now clear,
The music of the sea.
                    (JOYCE WINBOLT).

146

STORY SECTION

The Steps of the Master

Once upon a time, many years ago, Pierre the Fisherman set off one night to go fishing in his little boat. There was no moon and the night was dark as the little boat went bobbing on the waves far out to sea and, all alone, Pierre dropped his lines and waited for the fish. Suddenly, and without warning, there came the howling of the wind as a great storm arose. The rain lashed down and huge waves threatened to swamp his little boat. Fearing that he would be drowned, Pierre tried to make for home but the huge waves drove him nearer and nearer to the rocks at the foot of the cliffs. Soon he could hear the waves breaking against the jagged coast and, even in the darkness, could see the black cliffs towering above him. Then, a huge wave bigger than the rest lifted up his little boat and smashed it against the rocks and Pierre found himself clinging to the seaweed—breathless and half-drowned. Reaching up, he managed to clamber on to a slippery ledge and it seemed to him that his last moment had come for, below, the foaming waves threatened to sweep him away and above rose the high cliffs, black and forbidding.

There was no way of escape, but the fisherman was a man of faith and he prayed to God for help. Then, as he opened his eyes, he saw what seemed to him to be the shining figure of Jesus climbing up from the bottom of the cliff. Up and up He went, and it seemed to Pierre that wherever He put His foot to the ground, a step appeared, so that the way up the cliff was clearly marked. Pierre, planting his feet in the steps of the Master, steadily climbed to safety at the top of the cliff and ever after, even until today, that little island on the coast is called the Harbour of the Steps.

The Man who Sold his Shadow

There once lived a young man named Johann who, because he wanted to be rich and famous, was always grumbling. One fine, sunny day, when the sun was casting long shadows everywhere, he was walking along a hot and dusty street when he was stopped by a merchant.

147

'You have a fine shadow following you, young man,' said the merchant

'Have I?' replied Johann. 'Well the sun is low in the sky and September is the month of long shadows.' This he said, thinking that the man wanted something to talk about.

'I am buying shadows,' the merchant went on, 'and I would like to buy yours.' Johann thought that the man was joking so he said, 'Well, I don't think my shadow is of much use to me. What will you give me for it?'

The merchant thought for a moment, then he said, 'I haven't much money with me, but if you'll sign this paper saying that I can have your shadow, I will promise to make you rich and famous and the envy of all your friends.'

Still thinking he was joking, Johann agreed and signed the paper. The merchant took a pair of scissors from his pocket and quickly bent down. With a snip! snip! he neatly cut off Johann's shadow close to his heels and, rolling it up, stuffed it into a bag. With a strange chuckle, he raised his hat and walked away.

From that day, Johann became very rich and everything he touched turned to gold. At first he did not miss his shadow as he became famous and the envy of all his friends. Then people began to notice. 'That's strange!' they said 'The sun is shining and yet Johann has no shadow. Why can that be?' And they began to whisper among themselves and nudge each other as Johann walked by.

Johann began to notice what was going on and how people avoided him. He began to feel uncomfortable and to miss his shadow, jumping round quickly to see if it had returned. But no, nothing was there. He now began to stay in when the sun was out, and soon he grew so nervous that he stopped indoors, even when the day was dull and cloudy. At last, it became so bad that he sought out the merchant and begged for the return of his shadow.

'Yes,' said the merchant, 'but only in return for all the riches you have gained and everything that you have. Shadows, young man, as well as sunshine, are a part of our lives.'

The Day of the Rescue

Many years ago, there lived a girl named Grace Darling. She lived with her mother and father in a lighthouse, for her father was the lighthouse keeper and she helped him to keep the light always burning. It was a lonely life, for the lighthouse stood on the Farne Islands, flashing a warning to passing ships that dangerous rocks lay nearby on that part of the Northumberland coast.

148

One night in September, in the year 1838, a great storm arose in the North Sea and a small passenger ship on its way to Dundee was wrecked on the rocks some way away from the lighthouse. Most of the passengers on board were drowned, but when daylight came, Grace Darling could see a few of them still clinging to a rock but, every moment, they were in danger of being swept away by the huge waves. She begged her father to rescue them by rowing out in his boat.

'Father,' she pleaded, 'Let us go and save them. I am sure that we could reach them in our boat.'

At first, her father would not listen to her as he had only a small rowing boat called a coble. He could not row alone against the huge waves and strong tide without being swamped in such a tiny boat. But again, Grace pleaded with him.

'Let me go with you! You have taught me how to row and I am strong enough to pull on the oars.'

At last, her father agreed. 'Very well,' he said, 'we cannot leave them to drown. Help me to launch the boat.'

Quickly the boat was launched and, tossing like a cork on the enormous waves, father and daughter rowed out in the storm. Somehow, they got to the rock where nine people were clinging desperately for their lives. As the boat was so small they could take on board only five of them, four men and a woman, but another dangerous journey was made on the raging sea to rescue the remaining four and, at last, all nine were safely inside the lighthouse where they were cared for by Grace Darling and her mother.

The Church in a House

Once upon a time, nearly two thousand years ago, St. Paul the great missionary arrived at a seaport on the shores of Asia. He was very tired after his travels and that night, as he slept, he had a dream. In his dream a young man stood before him who was trying to tell him something. 'Come over and help us,' he seemed to be saying. 'Come over and help us.'

Now, across the water lay the great continent of Europe and Paul knew that God was calling him to spread the Good News of Jesus to other people. So, when he awoke the next morning, Paul said to his friends, 'Let us go down to the harbour and find a ship to carry us across the sea to the land that lays beyond.'

And, even though he had been travelling for many miles, often sick and ill, Paul that day boarded a ship and set sail.

Some days later, Paul arrived at the Roman city of Philippi and,

149

because it was the Sabbath, he looked for a church where he could worship God. But there were no churches in that city, nor anywhere in the whole country. Now the city stood between two rivers and Paul said to his friends. 'Perhaps if we go down to the riverside, we can find a quiet place to say our prayers,' and they walked through the city gates along the dusty lanes down to the cool riverside. By the river bank, in the shade of some trees, they saw a little group of women and Paul spoke to them.

'We are looking for a place to worship God,' he said.

'This is the only place we have,' said one of them, looking at the open sky and the trees. 'Will you join us?' So Paul and his friends joined them in their service and he talked to them about Jesus and His love for all people and how they could follow Him.

Afterwards, one of them named Lydia, a Greek woman who worshipped God, said to Paul, 'We would like to learn more about Jesus and to follow Him. I have a house in the city. Let us meet together in my house and you can tell us more about the Son of God.' And so it was that Lydia's house became the first church in Europe—the first church in the Western world.

The Calling of St. Matthew

In the time of Jesus, Roman soldiers tramped the highways of Palestine. Dressed in armour and carrying short swords, they treated the Jews very badly. On every busy road they placed a toll gate where merchants had to pay money before they could bring their goods into the city. Here sat the tax collector's or 'publicans' and sometimes they charged more than they should and kept the extra money for themselves. The Jews hated the Romans, but they hated the publicans even more.

One day, Jesus was passing the toll gate at the cross-roads of Capernaum, to the north of the Sea of Galilee. Merchants from Caesarea and Damascus and from far away Persia, were stopping to pay money in order to enter the city and piles of coins and bags of gold lay on the tables at the toll gate. Busily taking the money was the chief collector of taxes at Capernaum, a man named Levi who was very rich.

Jesus looked at him and saw a different man, a man who could be a faithful disciple. Very simply, Jesus said to him 'Follow me,' and, at once, Levi stood up and followed Him.

So happy was he at being chosen that Levi held a big feast in his house for Jesus. Among the guests he invited were his friends, tax collectors like himself and others who followed a bad way of life.

150

When the Pharisees saw this they said to the disciples, 'Why do you eat and drink with tax gatherers and sinners.' Jesus overheard them and answering, He said, 'It is not the healthy that need a doctor, but the sick; I have not come to invite virtuous people, but to call sinners to repentance.'

Levi became Matthew which means 'gift of God', and having made up his mind to follow Jesus he did not change it. He stayed with Jesus throughout His Life on earth and he was with the disciples at Pentecost when the gift of the Holy Spirit came upon them.

The Gift of the Rice Harvest

In the autumn, churches everywhere in England hold a Harvest Festival. People bring gifts of fruit and flowers and those gifts are sent to others who are in need. This story is about someone who gave not one small gift but everything he had to help others.

His name was Komoti and he lived many years ago in the island of Japan. His farm was on the slopes of a hill above a village on the sea shore and below him he could see the sparkling blue sea and the waves rolling over the yellow sand. Every year, he gathered in the harvest, the rice harvest of Japan, and he piled it in great stacks ready for the threshing.

Now, one Harvest Festival Day, Komoti was sitting alone at the door of his house looking down on the village below. The streets were gay with lanterns and banners for everyone was keeping the festival and Komoti was all alone in his house with Taro, his little grandson. Suddenly, Komoti felt the earth rock and tremble beneath his feet. It was an earthquake such as often comes to that part of the world. Everything seemed as usual in the village but then Komoti noticed that the sea was running away from the beach and the villagers were crowding on to the sea-shore to watch this strange happening. Looking out across the bay, Komoti could see a great wave gathering far out to sea and he knew that soon it would come sweeping back and all the villagers would be drowned.

'How can I call them away?' thought Komoti for he was high up on the hillside. Then an idea came to him and he called his grandson.

'Taro!' he cried, 'Fetch me a light from the fire!' Greatly wondering, little Taro brought a flaming branch from the fire and Komoti ran into his fields. Hurrying to the precious rice he stooped and set fire to a stack. He hastened to the next—and the next—and the next and soon all the rice stacks were blazing with red and yellow flames and clouds of thick black smoke went rolling up into the sky.

151

The people down on the beach saw the flames and clouds of smoke. 'Fire!' they shouted, and all began to hurry away from the sea-shore. Back they came to fight the fire, back they came to safety. Soon huge waves rolled on to the sea-shore and swept the beach where they had been standing. Anyone there would have been drowned, but all the villagers were now safely away from the beach—climbing the hill to fight the fire.

Komoti's rice was destroyed, but he had given his gift to the people for the Harvest Festival.

The Friendly Trees

At this time of the year, the trees shed their leaves so that they may grow again in the spring. But not all the trees lose their leaves for, so the story goes, God once saw a kindly deed.

One autumn, many years ago, the birds set off to seek the warmth and sunshine of the south. With a whirring of wings and much circling they gathered together and flew away from this land to seek the sun. All were winging their way southwards—all, except one. One sad, little bird fluttered alone as the days grew shorter. His friends had gone, leaving him behind, for his wing was broken and he could not fly for miles across the sea.

So, to the forest he came, begging for shelter and a resting place amongst the branches. But the trees were not friendly at all.

'Go away,' said the oak, with much rustling of his leaves, 'You will only eat my acorns.' So the little bird hopped away and went to the lime tree.

'There is no room for you here,' said the lime. 'I have far too many bees to look after.' Frightened and cold, the little bird went to the willow. But the willow was far too busy weeping even to lift her head. At last, sad and unhappy, the little bird tried to flutter away, but he only fell to the ground because of his broken wing. Then a voice called.

'Here, little stranger—I have a warm branch for you.' It was the kindly fir tree. Then the voice of the pine tree said, 'And I will shelter you from the cold North Wind.'

'My berries will give you food during the cold winter days,' called the holly, who was standing close by.

Glad at heart, the little bird hopped amongst the branches of these kindly trees and rested while its broken wing became stronger.

Soon Jack Frost began to spread his icy fingers through the forest and the North Wind came. He blew and blew the leaves from the unkind oak and lime and willow but God had seen the good deed of the kindly trees who had helped the little bird with the broken wing. And, to this day, they keep their leaves during the winter and are always evergreen.

Saint Jerome and the Lion

Long ago, there lived a good man named St. Jerome and, one day, as he sat at the gateway of the monastery, he was amazed to see a lion coming towards him. His friends jumped up and fled in terror but Jerome waited calmly. Then he saw that the lion was limping and, as he held up a swollen paw, Jerome could see a huge thorn sticking into the pad underneath. Gently he pulled it out and, after bathing the paw, he tried to drive the lion away. But, instead it settled down at his feet as if to say, 'I mean to stay here always.' The next morning, the lion was still laying on the floor beside him and followed him everywhere.

'Well!' said Jerome, 'If you mean to stay here you must work. No one can be idle. Every day you must go with my donkey into the forest and while the woodcutter loads the donkey with logs, you must stand guard and keep them safe from thieves and robbers.'

So, every morning, the lion went off with the donkey into the forest to keep watch and in the evening brought it safely home. But, one day when it was very hot, he grew drowsy and fell fast asleep under the trees. When he awoke, the donkey had gone and the woodcutter, too! Only the smell of men and the footprints of robbers told him that the donkey had been stolen.

Hanging his head with shame, the lion went back to the monastery. 'Where is the donkey?' asked Jerome sternly. 'I trusted you to keep watch and you have failed. Now, therefore, you must do its work and carry the logs on your own back.'

So, every morning, the lion went into the forest and in the evening he returned laden with logs on his back. Then, one day, a caravan was seen coming over the hills on its way to Egypt. There were camels laden with fine things from the East and men and horses and, at the head of the line—a donkey led by an old man.

Suddenly the lion lifted its head and sniffed the air. Then, up-setting the logs, he bounded forward with a glad roar for he had recognised the stolen donkey. The camel-drivers fled in terror but the lion bounded after them and drove them all into the monastery yard—merchants, camels, horses, and donkey. The noise was terrible, but when Jerome saw the donkey he understood what had happened. The merchants threw themselves down before the saint and confessed that they had stolen the donkey on the day the lion had slept. 'Forgive us this wrong,' they begged and Jerome, from the kindness of his heart, told them to go in peace.

So, once again, the lion and the donkey went out each day to the forest for firewood and in the evening the lion would crouch at the feet of St. Jerome and he stayed with him till the end of his days.

The House with the Golden Windows

Once upon a time, a little boy named Peter lived in a cottage on the side of a hill. His mother and father were very good to him and he had a little room of his own with gay curtains and a big cupboard full of toys. There were bright flowers in the garden where he used to play and, in one shady corner, a swing that his father had built for him. But, every evening, when the sun was low, he used to sit on the step outside the front door, his chin cupped in his hands, and gaze across the valley at a house on the other side. But this house was quite different from his. It had beautiful golden windows. Those windows shone so brightly that he never tired of looking at them and day after day he stared across at the house on the other side of the valley. 'How lucky the people are who live there,' he thought.

When he grew bigger and was old enough to go to school, he made up his mind to go and see that wonderful house with the windows of gold. So, one summer afternoon, he set off. He could hardly wait while his mother packed his sandwiches and a nice, cold drink for it promised to be a very hot day. Off he went down the hill with his eyes fixed on the house with the golden windows which looked even better than ever in the morning sun.

He thought he had not far to go but, as he trudged along the dusty road, the house seemed to get no nearer. On and on he went, down the valley and up the winding path on the other side. At last, very hungry and very tired, he arrived at the gate of the house and looked up. What a disappointment! It wasn't a wonderful house with golden windows, it was a cottage just like his own with glass windows.

Tired and hungry, Peter sat down to eat his sandwiches before starting back. It was getting late and the sun was going down. Rather unhappy, he looked across the valley and a wonderful sight met his eyes. It was a house with golden windows far more beautiful than the one he had seen before. It was his own house, and the sun was shining on the windows just as it had shone on those he had been looking at all these years.

'Well,' he thought, 'if only I'd thought of looking at my own windows, I wouldn't have come all this way for nothing'.

Brother Francis and the Wolf

There was once a good man named St. Francis who lived many years ago. Although he was rich, like the son of a prince, he gave up all his wealth and lived like a disciple of Jesus—helping the poor and healing the sick. He loved all wild creatures, the animals and the birds and, because he was so kind and gentle, they loved him too, and came at his call.

Once, he chanced to meet a man carrying doves in a cage, to be sold in the market. 'Do not cage them, I pray thee,' he begged, 'for they belong to the family of God.' At once, the man opened the cage and the doves fluttered out, settling on the shoulders of St. Francis for they had no fear of him.

When St. Francis stopped to speak beneath the trees, hundreds of birds flocked overhead and settled in the branches, some even brushing with their tiny wings the rough cloak that he wore. And, as he blessed them saying, 'Go in peace,' they spread their wings and, flying together, rose like a great cross in the sky.

In the evening, when the chattering of the swallows was so loud that his words could not be heard, he had but to raise his hand and say, 'Be silent, my little ones,' and at once their chattering ceased.

One day, Brother Francis came to a village where everyone was frightened. They were frightened to go anywhere because of a huge wolf that lived in the forest that attacked and killed all that it could find. As St. Francis came along, the men of the village, armed with sticks, were going out to hunt down the wolf and to kill it.

'Let me go and speak to Brother Wolf,' he begged.

'You will only be killed,' they scoffed, but St. Francis set off into the forest alone and unarmed. When he came near to the wolf's den, the animal sprang out as if to leap upon him. But Francis had no fear. 'Come hither, Brother Wolf,' he called 'Do me no harm,' and, at once, the wolf came meekly and lay down at his feet. When St. Francis returned to the village, the wolf followed him like a dog. No longer did it kill but it became a friend of the village, begging its food from door to door and being fed by them all. They called it 'Brother Wolf' because they remembered the words of St. Francis when he said 'All birds and animals belong to God's great family.'

Columbus finds the New World

In the sunny land of Italy, more than four hundred years ago, there lived a boy named Christopher Columbus. His father was a weaver and young Christopher often used to help him with his work. At school, he had to learn Latin and mathematics and all about the stars but, during playtimes, he loved to wander down to the harbour and watch the tall masts of strange ships from far away countries across the sea. As he listened to the stirring tales of the seamen he decided that he, too, would become a sailor and explore the world. So, at the age of 14, he became a seaman.

When he grew up, Columbus longed to find a new way to the rich countries of the East. One day, as he was looking at some old maps, he decided that the east could be reached by sailing to the west, because the earth was round. To get the ships he needed, Columbus went to the King and Queen of Spain and, after many years of pleading, they gave him three ships for his voyage—the *Santa Maria*, the *Nina*, and the *Pinta*.

So one sunny day in August the three ships weighed anchor and sailed out into the Atlantic. They called it the Sea of Darkness and as they sailed on and on, further than anyone before, the men began to be afraid. 'We shall be blown over the edge of the world', they said. 'Let us go back,' and they even plotted to throw Columbus overboard if he did not return.

But Columbus was not afraid. By keeping two log books he made them think they were nearer home than they were and he offered a reward of a bag of gold and a velvet suit to the first one who sighted land. At last, he had to promise that if land was not seen within three days, they would turn back.

Then, on October 11th, they found a branch covered with berries floating in the water and that night Columbus saw a tiny light in the distance as if a fire was burning on a shore. Early the next morning, the booming of a cannon from the *Pinta* told them all that land had been sighted and, as dawn came, they saw the low lying shores of an island.

On that October day, Columbus landed in the New World of America. At once he knelt down on the sandy beach and gave thanks to God for His great mercy and for keeping them safe on their great voyage across the sea.

The Good Samaritan

One day, when Jesus and His friends were walking towards Jerusalem, a young man came up to Him and tried to test Jesus with this question. 'Master, what must I do to gain eternal life?'

Knowing that the man was a lawyer, Jesus said to him, 'What does the Law tell you to do?'

Quickly, the young man replied, 'Love the Lord your God with all your heart, with all your soul, with all your strength, and with all your mind; and your neighbour as yourself.'

'That is the right answer,' said Jesus; 'do that and you will live.'

But the young man, wanting to show off in front of the crowd, asked another question, 'Yes, but who is my neighbour?' Jesus answered him by telling the story of the Good Samaritan.

A man was on his way from Jerusalem down to Jericho. It was a dangerous road, shut in by high rocks and dark caves where robbers lay in wait to pounce upon all who travelled alone. Suddenly and without warning, the man was set upon by a band of robbers who stripped him, beat him, and then ran off leaving him half dead.

As the man lay on the road, wounded and unable to move, he heard footsteps. By chance, a Priest was going down to Jericho by that same road, but when he saw the wounded man he crossed over to the other side and hurried past—perhaps frightened at what might happen to him if he stayed to help.

Sick at heart, the wounded man lay helpless and suffering, for very few people passed that way and it was getting dark. Then he heard footsteps again. This time it was a Levite, a servant of the temple but he, too, crossed the road and passed by on the other side.

Then came the sound of hoofs as a Samaritan came riding by on his donkey. The wounded man gave a groan, for if a priest and a Levite would not help, what chance would he stand with a foreigner. But then he felt gentle hands lifting him up, bandaging his wounds and bathing them with oil and wine. He felt himself lifted on to the back of a donkey and soon came to an inn where the Samaritan gave the innkeeper two silver coins, saying as he did so, 'Look after him; and if you spend any more, I will repay you on my way back.'

When Jesus had finished the story, He turned to the lawyer who had been asking the questions and said, 'Which of these three do you think was neighbour to the man who fell into the hands of the robbers?'

The lawyer replied, 'The one who showed him kindness.' Then Jesus said, 'Go and do as he did.'

Hans the Shepherd Boy

Hans was a little shepherd boy who lived in Germany. One day, when he was keeping his master's sheep, a hunter rode up to him out of the forest.

'How far is it to the nearest village, my boy?' asked the hunter.

'It is six miles, sir,' replied Hans. 'But the road is only a sheep track. You might easily miss your way.'

'My boy,' said the hunter, leaning down from his horse, 'if you will take me there I will pay you well.'

Hans shook his head. 'I cannot leave the sheep, sir,' he said. 'They would stray into the forest and the wolves might eat them.'

'But if one or two sheep are lost or eaten,' said the hunter 'I will pay you well for them. I will give you more than you can earn in a year.'

'No, sir', said Hans. 'The sheep belong to my master. If they are lost, I should be to blame.'

'If you cannot take me to the village,' the hunter went on, 'will you get me a guide? I will take care of your sheep while you are gone.'

Again Hans shook his head. 'I cannot do that,' he said. 'The sheep do not know your voice and I do not know if you will take good care of them.'

'Can't you trust me?' asked the hunter. ·

'No, sir,' said Hans. 'You have tried to make me break my promise to my master; how do I know that you will keep your promise to me.'

The hunter laughed. 'You are right,' he said. 'I wish I could trust my servants as your master can trust you.'

Just then several men rode out of the forest and seeing the hunter they spurred their horses towards him.

'Sire!' they shouted joyfully. 'We thought you were lost!'

Then Hans learned to his great surprise that the hunter was a prince of the kingdom. He was afraid that the great man would punish him. But the prince only smiled and spoke in praise of him and then they all rode away.

Some days later a servant came from the prince and took Hans to the palace.

'Hans,' said the prince, 'I want you to leave your sheep and to come and serve me. I know that you are a boy whom I can trust.'

Hans was very happy over his good fortune but he replied, 'If my master can find another boy to take my place, then I will come and serve you.'

So Hans went back and looked after the sheep until his master found another boy. After that he served the prince for many years.

The Storm on the Sea of Galilee

It was evening when Jesus came to the shores of the Sea of Galilee. Throughout the long day He had been teaching and healing and still the great crowds pressed around Him, eager to listen to His words.

Right down to the beach they went to where the boats were pulled up on the sandy shore. Jesus climbed into one of the boats and sat there talking to the crowds, as the water lapped against their feet.

Now many of the disciples were fishermen, skilled in the handling of boats and, as it was getting so late, Jesus beckoned to them and said, 'Let us cross over to the other side of the lake.'

The crowds, seeing that He was about to leave, made a rush for the other boats so that they could follow Him wherever He went. Quickly, the disciples slid the boat into deep water and, hoisting the triangular sail, they steered for the opposite shore.

Worn out with His day of teaching and healing, Jesus stretched Himself out in the stern, or back, of the boat and was soon sound asleep on a cushion that lay there.

There is no twilight in the East and the night comes suddenly. Now it was quite dark and all was peaceful and quiet on the lake. The other boats had gone and the darkness had blotted out the shore. Soon, only a few lights gleamed from the lakeside villages and the stars twinkled overhead. Only the sound of the waves lapping against the side of the boat and the creak of the sail could be heard. The disciples talked in whispers so as not to waken their Master.

The boat was a long way from the shore when, suddenly, Peter looked up in alarm. Heavy clouds had hidden the stars and the wind was howling across the lake. Soon, great waves crashed over the boat, swamping it, and it looked as if they were going to sink. All this time Jesus slept and the disciples, although they were fishermen and used to storms, became very frightened.

'Master!' they shouted, 'we are sinking! Do you not care?'

It was only then that Jesus stood up and, speaking as much to the disciples as He did to the storm and the sea, He said, 'Hush! Be still!' At once the storm ceased as suddenly as it had begun. The wind dropped and there was a dead calm.

Jesus turned to His disciples, 'Why are you such cowards?' he said, 'Have you no faith even now?'

The disciples were overcome with wonder and they whispered to one another, saying, 'Who can this be whom even the wind and the sea obey?'

Christ of the Andes

This story is about two countries existing side by side with only high mountains in between them. Now the people who lived in the two countries were always quarrelling about the land on the sides of

159

the mountains—each country claiming it for its own. At last they said, 'We will go to war and fight for the land.' So they built forts on the mountains with big guns and soldiers to shoot anyone who came that way.

But there lived two holy men, one in each country, and they were very sad that there should be fighting. So each man travelled his own country, going from village to village and town to town, pleading with the people not to go to war. At last they were successful and everybody agreed that they would live in peace.

'But,' said one holy man, 'suppose they forget and start quarrelling all over again. Who will help them to remember when we are gone?' Then a thought from God came into his mind.

'Let us build a statue of Jesus high up in the mountains, between the two countries, so that they will always remember and keep the peace in His name.'

So the great bronze guns of war were melted down and the metal was taken to a sculptor who made it into a statue of Jesus. It was placed on a train and taken to the foot of the high, snowy mountains which lie between the two countries. Then a band of soldiers and sailors from both countries carried the statue up the steep mountain road. Up and up they went until the road was so high that it was covered with ice and snow, thirteen thousand feet above the sea. There they set the statue up on a huge block of stone cut from the mountain side and they sent a message to the people of both countries—'Come, the statue is ready.'

So they came and there, above them all, was the figure of Jesus. One of His hands held a cross and the other was stretched out to bless the world and beneath Him were the words: 'He is our peace Who hath made both one.' And the people were glad that they had met together and were friends once again.

The statue is still there today, high up in the mountains. The mountains are called the Andes and the statue stands between the two countries of Argentina and Chile in South America and their peoples have kept the peace in the name of Jesus ever since that day.

A Prince Learns to Read

Once upon a time the Queen of Wessex was in her palace watching her three sons, the young princes, playing together. 'One day,' the Queen thought to herself, 'one of these boys will be the King of Wessex. I hope that whoever is King will be good and wise, as well as brave.'

The Queen rose from her stool and took down a large book from a shelf. Opening it carefully, she called to the three princes. 'Come, my sons, and see this treasure of mine.'

The three boys gathered round their mother, and looked at the book. They could not read it, of course, because in those days there were not many books and few people could read, but they liked the pictures and the coloured letters.

As the Queen turned the pages, the boys pointed to the pictures with delight and wanted to know what the stories were about.

'If you could read, my sons,' said the Queen, 'you would know that this is the Bible and the stories are more wonderful than the pictures. This is God's book, and in it are the stories I have told you of Joseph and his coat of many colours, of David and Goliath, and of Jesus in the manger and of His wonderful life on earth. Listen, my sons,' the Queen went on, 'I will give this book to the first of you who is able to read it.'

At first, the boys worked hard to win the prize but, soon, the eldest prince grew tired. 'Who wants to learn to read?' he said. 'I'm going out to practise with my new spear. Kings need to fight, not read.' So he stopped learning.

Then the second prince became lazy. 'Why should I stay indoors looking at all these words while, outside, the sun is shining.' So he, too, stopped learning.

Now only the youngest prince was left making the shapes of the letters and saying their sounds. His name was Alfred and he, too, liked throwing the spear and playing in the sunshine as much as his brothers, but he was wise as well as brave and he kept on trying and trying. Then came the exciting day when he could read.

Once more the Queen went to the shelf and took down the great book. Opening it carefully, she called the princes to her. The eldest prince put down his spear and came to look at the pictures, but as the Queen pointed to the words he shook his head. Then the second prince tried but he, too, could not understand what the words had to say. Now, it was Alfred's turn.

As the Queen pointed to the words, he began to read. Slowly and carefully at first, but then better and better until he was reading the wonderful stories. At last, the Queen closed the book. 'Well done, Alfred,' she said, 'you have worked hard to win the prize. The book is yours.'

When Alfred grew up, he became the King of Wessex. He fought the Danes, defeated them in battle and then made peace with them. He was the first king who tried to make his people good and wise. And the people loved him and called him Alfred the Great—the only English King to be called the Great.

Michelangelo

One day, many years ago, a boy was born. It was on a Sunday, so his father thought that he would name him after an angel, the angel Michael. Or, in Italian, Michelangelo—and that was his name.

Michelangelo grew up and went to school. He was not very good at sums, but at painting pictures he was very good indeed. His father became very angry with him.

'You are wasting your time,' he said, 'you must work for a living.' So at the age of 13 Michelangelo was sent to work for a great artist. The artist showed him how to mix the colours and clean the brushes and gave him a picture to copy. The copy was so good that no one could tell which was the real picture when they were placed side by side.

'This boy knows more than I do,' said the artist, and Michelangelo had to leave.

Although he was so good at painting, Michelangelo really wanted to become a sculptor. He even made statues out of ice and snow, which were wonderful—until the sun came out and they melted away.

In the city where he lived was a huge block of marble. For forty years it had been lying outside a cathedral and many had tried to carve something from it, without success. Michelangelo stood in front of the great, white marble block and thought for a long while. Then he took up his chisel and began to work. Two years later, his task was done and people came to see it. To their surprise, instead of the shapeless block of marble, there was a wonderful statue of David the Shepherd Boy. Everyone flocked to see the statue and many artists were rather jealous and came to find fault with it.

Said one of them, 'The nose is too big for the face. It would be better if you altered it.' Michelangelo said nothing although he knew it was all right. Instead, he climbed the scaffolding (for the statue was 12 feet high) and pretended to tap with his chisel. Then he sprinkled some marble dust on the head of the artist below, and came down.

'Is that better?' he asked gravely, 'Much better,' said the artist, 'Now you have given it life.'

The fame of Michelangelo spread until he was asked by the Pope of Rome to paint pictures on the ceiling of a great chapel. It meant that he would have to work lying on his back, at the top of a scaffold, many dizzy feet above the floor. He set to work with his paints. The ceiling measured 5,000 square feet and he painted 145 pictures telling stories from the Bible. For four and a half years he worked, with his head thrown back for hours, painting on the ceiling above

162

him. And, on the 1 November 1512, his great work was finished for all the world to enjoy.

The Bell in the Market Place

Once upon a time, in a little town in Italy, there hung a bell in the market place. Over the bell there was a little wooden roof and tied to the bell there was a rope. It was a gift from the king to the people and he said to them. 'This bell is yours. It must only be rung when any of you have suffered harm or injury. When the bell rings out, we will know that a wrong has been done and all will come to your aid to give you justice.'

The bell hung in the market place for many years and it was always rung by those who needed help and everyone was very pleased with it.

After a time, the rope became very worn and frayed and a passer-by, seeing this, cut a grape-vine that was growing near-by. Tying the leafy stalk to the bell, so that even a child could reach it, he went on his way.

Now it happened that in the town there lived a knight who had once been gallant and brave, but now he cared only for money, and gold became the only thing he wanted. He sold his armour, his horses, and his hounds; and he kept only one old horse to starve and shiver in the stable.

Every day, the knight tried to save more money so that he could add to his sacks of gold. At last he said to himself, 'Why should I keep that old horse in the stable, eating food night and day. I'll turn him out and he can find food for himself.'

And so, without a thought for the poor animal that had served him so well and had grown old and blind, he turned him out of the stable to wander in the lanes and fields, barked at by the dogs and torn by the briars.

Now, one hot afternoon when all the people of the town were either dozing or fast asleep, everyone was suddenly awakened by the ringing of the bell. The magistrate sat up and, putting on his robes, he hurried to the market place. The crowds followed after him but, as they came near to the bell, all they could see was the old horse. Hungry and sightless, he had brushed against the grape-vine tied to the bell and was nibbling at the leaves. As he pulled on the leaves, the bell rang out.

'Good gracious me,' said the magistrate. 'This horse belongs to the knight. He rings the bell as loudly as the rest and calls for justice in his deep distress.'

Meanwhile, a great crowd had gathered as the news spread through the town. 'The horse needs our help,' they said, 'justice must be done.' So they found the cruel knight who had been so unfair, and they made him take back the horse that had served him so well, to care for it for the rest of its days.

The Little Girl who would not Work

There was once a little girl who loved to play all day out of doors among the flowers and the trees. Her mother thought she would grow into a lazy little girl if she played so much. 'You are old enough to do some work,' she said to her daughter. 'Even when you are young you can learn to be busy.'

But the little girl said, 'Oh, mother, I don't like to work. Please let me go into the woods and play just a little while longer.' So her mother said she could play, but only for a little while.

The child ran out of the house, and across the garden, and down to the woods as fast as her feet could carry her. As she hurried on, a Red Squirrel jumped across her path and the little girl said to him, 'Red Squirrel, you don't have to work, do you? You just play, and eat nuts from morning till night.'

'Not work!' chattered the Red Squirrel, 'why, I am working now, and I worked all day yesterday and the day before. My family lives in the old oak tree and, for them, I must store away nuts for the winter. I have no time to stop and play.'

Just then a Bee came buzzing by and the little girl said, 'Little Bee, do you have any work to do?'

'Work!' buzzed the Bee, 'why, I am always working, gathering sweets and making the honeycomb for you. I have no time for play.'

The little girl walked along very slowly, for she was thinking, and she saw an Ant, down on the path, carrying a very large crumb of bread. 'That crumb of bread is too heavy for you, Ant,' she said, 'drop it, and come and play with me.'

'I don't care how heavy it is,' said the Ant, 'I was so glad to find it that I am willing to carry it. Oh no, I couldn't stop to play.' And on went the Ant with his crumb of bread.

So the little girl sat down upon a stone, to think better, and she said to herself. 'The creatures all have something to do, but I don't believe the flowers work. Do you work, Pink Clover?' she asked a little flower growing at her feet.

'Indeed I do,' said the Pink Clover. 'Every day I gather sunbeams in my petals and search for water with my roots to get ready for seed time. The flowers must all work.'

164

Then the little girl ran home to her mother and said, 'Mother, the Squirrels and the Bees and the Ants and the Flowers all have work to do. Have you got some for me?'

So her mother gave her an apron which the little girl had begun to hem so long ago that she had forgotten all about it; and she was so busy with her needle that she also forgot to be idle any more.

St. Martin, the Good Soldier

There was once a good man named St. Martin. His parents were heathen and did not believe in God, and when Martin was only 15 years old he had to follow his father into the Roman army and become a soldier.

One day, Martin was riding through France on horseback, wearing the plumed helmet, armour, and cloak of a Roman soldier. It was a bitterly cold day and a keen wind was blowing the snow in gusts about him. As he came riding up to the gates of a city, a poor beggar lying by the roadside lifted up his arms and cried, 'Have pity, ye sons of Rome! In the name of your gods—have pity!'

The other Roman soldiers, who were with Martin, laughed and spurring their horses they rode past spattering the beggar with mud. But Martin reined in his horse and stopped.

'I have nothing to give you,' he said. Then, looking with pity upon the old man shivering by the wayside, he threw off his red cloak and drawing his sword, cut the cloak in two and gave half to the beggar. Without a backward glance, Martin rode away.

That night, while asleep in his tent, Martin had a dream. In his dream he saw the figure of Jesus, but there was something different. The figure of Christ was wearing a torn cloak—the half cloak that had been given to the beggar.

When Martin awoke, he thought about his dream and he decided to become a Christian. Two years went by before Martin was able to leave the army, and he became a monk and travelled afar preaching the word of God.

He reached a country where there were many heathens who worshipped idols. One of the idols was a huge pine tree and Martin knew that they would never turn from their evil ways until the tree was cut down. So he gave the order to chop down the tree but, as he did so, armed men came forward to kill him. As they came closer, Martin called to them.

'If you think that I am doing wrong by cutting down your god, the pine tree,' he called, 'bind me and place me where the tree will fall. Then cut it down and let the tree, your god, punish me.'

As these men were from the forests and could make a tree fall exactly where it was wanted, they agreed, and binding Martin they placed him where the tree would fall. Then the sound of axes rang through the forest and the huge tree tottered and fell with a crash. But, to their amazement, it fell the other way and Martin was unhurt.

St. Martin lived to bring Christianity to many countries and, today, there are churches named after him all over the world.

The Monastery on the Island

Once, long ago, there were some holy men called monks who lived on a rocky, little island off the coast of France. They grew their own vegetables and did all their own work. In fact, they were the only people on the island.

One night, one of the monks called Anselm had a dream. He dreamed that they were being told to build a monastery right on top of the island mountain. It would be a fine place for it. Anselm knew that, even in his dream. People would see it for miles, and it would be a sign of the God they worshipped.

Next morning, Anselm went and looked at the place and saw how rocky it was. He still thought it would be a fine place, but the monks would never be able to move all those stones and Anselm shook his head. But the next night he had the same dream, and again the third night, so he told the others.

They all agreed that it would be difficult, but because of Anselm's threefold dream, they began to clear a space on the top of the island. Some stones they wanted, others they rolled down the hillside. Some went splash! into the sea. But there was one stone they could not move. Try as they would, it stayed firm and they were in despair. Then Anselm had another dream. He dreamed that, on the mainland, there was a farmer who had seven sons, and they were all helping the monks to move the stone.

In the morning, Anselm rowed across to the mainland where he found the farmer who had the seven sons. Yes, they would all come and help, and they rowed back to the island. Up the hill they went and, with the monks, they pushed the stone. They pulled and pushed —but it did not move.

'That's strange,' said Anselm, and then he noticed that there were only six sons. 'Are there not seven of you?' he asked.

'Yes,' replied the farmer, 'but I did not bring the youngest. He is only a bit of a boy and has no strength. It was not worth bringing him.'

'Nay,' said Anselm, 'there were seven in my dream and seven it must be.'

So the six sons went back to the mainland and came next morning with the youngest brother. As they had said, he was only 'a bit of a boy' with very little strength. But, when they all pushed at the stone together, over it went and toppled down the hillside.

The youngest boy's strength was not just 'a little bit'—it was 'a little bit more.'

The Moonlight Sonata

One winter evening, Beethoven the great writer of music, and his friend, were walking along the cobbled streets of a town in Germany. As they passed by a poor cottage in a narrow street, Beethoven stopped and listened. 'Hush,' he said to his friend, 'what sound is that?'

From the cottage, they could hear someone playing the piano and Beethoven had recognised the music that he had written.

Suddenly, the music stopped and then they heard the sound of a girl crying, 'I can play no more,' the voice went on, 'how I wish I could hear the music played at a great concert.'

To the surprise of his friend, Beethoven tapped at the door of the cottage. 'I am going in,' he said.

'Why?' said the other.

'I will play for her,' replied the great composer, and, lifting the latch, he went in. Inside, the cottage was poor and lit only by a candle. They saw a cobbler mending shoes and a young girl sitting at the piano. Apologising for his entry, Beethoven said to the girl, 'I am a musician and could not help hearing what you said. May I play for you?'

'You are welcome,' said the cobbler. 'But our piano is old and wretched and we have no music.'

'No music!' exclaimed Beethoven, 'then how does this young lady play—?' Then he stopped suddenly for, as the girl turned her head, he saw that she was blind.

Beethoven apologised and then sat down to play as he had never played before. The others in the room, forgetting everything except the wonderful music, sat listening until the candle spluttered and went out, plunging the room into darkness. Beethoven strode to the window and threw open the shutters to let the moonlight flood into the room. The cobbler, thinking that he had finished, said to him, 'Who are you?'

'Listen,' said Beethoven and he played the opening bars of his music that the girl had been trying to play.

167

'Then you are Beethoven!' said the cobbler with delight. Then, in the moonlight, Beethoven began to play a new piece of music. Slow at first, then quick like the dance of fairies. When he had finished, Beethoven left them, after promising to come back and help the blind girl, and hurrying home he sat down to write out the music that he had been playing.

Before dawn broke, Beethoven had finished the music to his satisfaction. And so it was, through helping a blind girl, that Beethoven wrote his wonderful *Moonlight Sonata* which has given the world so much pleasure ever since.

The White Feather of Friendship

In the early days of the Pilgrim Fathers, the Red Indians were not always friendly and, one day, news came that they were on the war-path—killing the settlers and burning their log cabins. Now, they were coming nearer to a settlement where, among others, lived a Pilgrim with his wife and two small children.

As soon as news of the danger reached them, the settlers decided to leave and ride off to a fort some miles away where they would be safe. In a short time, the place was deserted.

But the Pilgrim did not ride off. He stayed because he did not believe in fighting and because he trusted in God. When every other cabin was empty, his own sheltered all he held most dear. When everywhere else was quiet, there was the sound of children playing in his log-dwelling—but this stopped when they went to bed. For an hour or two after dark, the Pilgrim and his wife went on with their work by lamplight, and when all was finished they retired for the night. The Pilgrim, as usual, drawing in the latch-thong (a strip of leather which hung outside the door) so that no one could come in by pulling it down and so raising the latch.

After a time, however, he said, 'Wife, ought we not to have left the latch-thong outside? Surely God can protect us, if it be His will, without our fastening the door.'

'You know best,' she replied, frightened though she must have been. So the Pilgrim opened the door, drew out the latch-thong, and left it hanging limply outside, ready for all who cared to come in. Then he went to bed.

He was awakened, not by any sound, but by a sense that all was not well. Going to the window he looked out and, there in the moon-light, were dark figures gliding among the cabins. The Indians had come—only to find the place empty and they were angry. One by one, the log cabins were set on fire.

Stepping back into the room, the Pilgrim stood still hardly daring to breathe. Suddenly, two eyes appeared at the window and a face pressed against the glass. Other eyes looked in; there were shouts and yells and the sound of bare feet running round the cabin. They had been seen. With a whispered prayer, the Pilgrim stood back, waiting for them to rush the door. How long he stood there he never knew and then, unable to bear it any longer, he strode across the cabin and wrenched open the door expecting a hundred arrows.

Not an Indian was in sight. At first, the Pilgrim could not believe his eyes, but presently he glanced up and there, nodding faintly in the breeze, was a white feather in the thatched roof. It was the Red Indian sign of friendship. They had replied to his courage in their own way.

Fishers of Men

It was morning on the shores of the Sea of Galilee. The sea lapped against the beach and boats were bobbing on the waves as two fishermen, who were brothers, worked to mend their nets on the sea-shore. As their strong hands moved over the nets, making good the holes that had been torn by the rocks, they talked quietly together as if fearing to be overheard.

'Have you seen Him again, Andrew?' said one.

'Not since I told you about Him, Simon,' replied his brother. 'Not since I saw Him with John the Baptist by the River Jordan.' The two brothers fell silent as they bent to their work.

'Tell me again what happened,' whispered Simon eagerly.

'I was standing with John, the one who baptizes, when this man Jesus passed by. John looked towards Him and said, "There is the Lamb of God". We heard him say this clearly as we were standing so close.'

'Do you really think He is the Leader sent by God?' asked Simon. 'Because I would follow Him to the end if He led us to fight against our Roman masters.'

At that moment, a company of Roman soldiers marched by, roughly ordering people out of the way, and Simon's face was black with anger as he looked at them.

'I don't think the New Leader wants us to fight,' said Andrew slowly. 'Perhaps the Kingdom of God will come in some other way. But come!' he said suddenly. 'The net is finished. Let us go fishing.'

Quickly the two brothers stripped to the waist, as was the custom in the east and, wading into the sea, cast their net upon the water. In a short while, the net was full of silvery fish, leaping and wriggling,

169

and they hauled it towards the shore. One of the brothers swam behind, diving occasionally to ease the net over the rocks.

So busy were they, that they did not notice what was happening on the shore behind them. It was Simon, always quick to act, who saw the crowd first.

'Quick, Andrew!' he called to his brother, 'it is the Messiah, the New Leader, with the crowds around Him.' Turning from their fine haul of fish, the brothers began to wade towards the land when, suddenly, they heard a voice—the voice of Jesus. He had seen them fishing and was now calling to them from the shore.

'Come with me,' He said, 'and I will make you fishers of men.'

As quickly as possible, Andrew and Simon waded to the beach. Throwing down their net full of fish and leaving their boat and everything behind them, they went off to follow Jesus.

The Gifts in the Night

Once, long ago, there lived a good man called St. Nicholas. As a young man he was very rich, but he cared nothing for money and he made up his mind to use his wealth to help the poor. Not to give it away to anyone, but to give where the need was greatest.

Now, in the town, there lived a poor man with his three daughters and, one day, as Nicholas passed by their cottage he heard the sound of crying. He stopped and listened as he heard a girl's voice, saying, 'Father, let us go into the streets to beg for food as we are so hungry and it is hard to starve.'

Then Nicholas heard the father answer, 'Not just yet. Let us wait for one more night and I will pray to God for help.'

Nicholas hurried away for he knew that in his treasure chest he had three bags of gold. That night, when everyone was fast asleep, he returned to the cottage. Snow was falling as he reached the home of the poor man and his three daughters and, looking up, he saw a hole in the wall that served as a chimney. By standing on tiptoe, he could just reach it and he dropped the bag of gold into the opening where it fell upon the cold and empty hearth. Then Nicholas hurried away, his footsteps making no sound upon the fallen snow.

In the morning, the poor man was amazed to find a bag of gold by the fireplace and, not knowing from whence it came, he gave thanks to God for their unknown friend.

The next night, Nicholas came again to the cottage and dropped another bag of gold for the second daughter through the opening and, as secretly as he came, he hurried away.

On the third night, the poor man made up his mind to keep watch, so he crept out and hid himself near the cottage. As soon as it was dark, he heard the sound of quiet footsteps and St. Nicholas passed by and dropped the third bag of gold into the opening in the cottage wall.

Running quickly from his hiding place, the poor man seized Nicholas by his red robe and, kneeling at his feet, cried, 'O Nicholas, servant of God, why do you seek to hide yourself?'

'It is my way of making others happy. I pray you to tell no one, not even your daughters, but give thanks to God for it was He who sent me to you.'

This and many other gifts of kindness did St. Nicholas do in the name of God and always in secret. He is the favourite saint of children because, in Holland, they call St. Nicholas Santa Claus and, now, children all over the world hang up their stockings by the fireplace in the hope that Santa Claus will fill them with presents on Christmas Eve.

The First Christmas Tree

At the time when the Christ Child was born all the people, the animals, and the trees, and the plants were very happy. The Child was born to bring peace and happiness to the whole world. People came every day to see the little One, and they always brought gifts with them.

There were three trees standing near the stable which saw the people and they wished that they, too, might give presents to the Christ Child.

The Palm said, 'I will choose my most beautiful leaf, and place it as a fan over the Child.'

'And I,' said the Olive tree, 'will sprinkle sweet-smelling oil upon His head.'

'What can I give to the Child?' asked the Fir tree who stood near.

'You!' cried the others, 'you have nothing to offer Him. Your leaves prick like needles and your tears are sticky.'

So the poor little Fir tree was very unhappy and said, 'Yes you are right. I have nothing to offer the Christ Child.'

Now, quite near the trees stood the Christmas Angel, who had heard all that the trees had said. The Angel was sorry for the Fir tree who was so meek and without envy of the other trees. So, when it was dark and the stars came out, he begged a few of the little stars to come down and rest upon the branches of the Fir tree. They did as the Christmas Angel asked, and the Fir tree shone suddenly with a beautiful light.

171

And, at that very moment, the Christ Child opened His eyes—for he had been asleep—and as the lovely light fell upon Him He smiled.

Every year people keep the birthday of Jesus by giving gifts to each other and every year, in remembrance of His first birthday, there is a brightly lit and shining fir tree at Christmas time in many houses. Covered with twinkling lights it shines upon the happy faces of boys and girls as the stars shone for the Christ Child. The Fir tree was rewarded for its meekness, for to no other tree is it given to shine upon so many happy faces.

The Journey to Bethlehem

Early one morning, before the sun was up, Mary and Joseph got ready to start on their journey. Joseph chose a staff to help him on the way, and Mary took a cloak and a woollen wrap to put over her head. The little donkey waited in the yard and, when all was ready, Joseph helped Mary into the saddle. Down the village street they went, before anyone else was about, and the donkey's hooves clattered over the stony cobbles.

They journeyed on all day and, when night came, Joseph made a fire of sticks which he had gathered, and Mary took food from Joseph's leather bag for the evening meal. Afterwards the grey donkey was tied up nearby, and the two travellers wrapped their long cloaks about them and slept under the stars.

By the ninth day, Mary and Joseph and even the grey donkey were very tired, for the way had been long with many hills and stony places to cross. But, at last, the little town of Bethlehem came into sight.

'Soon we shall find shelter and a warm place to sleep for the night,' said Joseph. 'The inn at Bethlehem is comfortable, and the innkeeper is a kindly man.'

But as they got nearer to the town gate they saw many people crowding through. And when they had passed through the gate they found the streets packed with other travellers newly arrived.

'They have all come at the King's order as we have,' said Joseph.

He led the way to the inn, and helped Mary down from the donkey. How glad she was to have reached the end of the journey at last! But when the innkeeper saw them, he shook his head. 'So many travellers have come that I have no room in the inn,' he said.

'We are very weary,' said Joseph. 'We have thick cloaks and a mat, if only you will give us a place to lie down in the warm.'

'Come in,' said the innkeeper, 'I will show you all that I have left.' His long guest room was filled with guests. There was no room there. He led them to the end of it and down three steps. Now they were in the stable. Two great oxen lay on the floor and high up in the dark corners some hens and pigeons were roosting. 'This is the only place left,' said the innkeeper, 'but it's warm, and there is plenty of clean, sweet hay.'

Mary and Joseph were only too glad to stay there. Joseph led in their grey donkey, and then spread fresh hay for Mary to lie on, and covered her with his cloak. Presently everything grew quiet in the stable and, outside, the whole world lay still and peaceful under the twinkling stars.

The Silver Cones

It was ten days to go until Christmas Day and the children were decorating the Christmas tree. Their mother looked up from her work and said to them, 'Why don't you hang some silver cones on the tree like the mountain folk?'

'Why do they do that?' asked the children, altogether.

'Well,' she replied, 'it happened like this.'

Once, a long time ago in the mountains, there lived a poor maiden named Gretchen. She was very poor for her parents had died when she was very young, and she had to look after all the other children in the family. As Christmas Day was soon to come, she wondered how she could buy presents and sweets for them all.

So, one evening when it was very cold, Gretchen started out for the forest to gather some pine cones. As it was so cold, she hoped to sell the pine cones for fuel, and perhaps get some money.

Now, in the forest there lived a man called Rubezahl, who had magic powers and looking out of the tiny window of his wooden hut, he saw Gretchen wandering among the trees.

'What are you doing?' he called in his squeaky voice.

'I've come to gather pine cones to sell for fuel,' replied Gretchen. And then she told him how she hoped to buy gifts for the children because they were so poor.

Now Rubezahl was a kind old man and, thinking hard he rubbed his silver beard. Then, pointing to the great fir tree, the little man said, 'Over there you will find the best pine cones. But mind you gather the largest if you hope to sell them!' And with a strange little chuckle, the old man disappeared.

Sure enough the pine cones lay thick upon the great fir tree and Gretchen gathered a basket full to the brim. As she walked home along the forest path, the basket grew heavier and heavier until, at last, when she reached the hut where she lived, she could hardly lift it over the front doorstep.

'Come and see my lovely cones!' she called to the children. As they peeped into the basket, they saw a gleam brighter than moonbeams, for every pine cone had turned into pure silver. There was enough to buy presents for all the children and to live in comfort for the rest of their lives.

'And that is why the mountain folk hang silver cones on their Christmas trees,' said mother. 'Now let's finish ours.'

The Lonely Shepherd

Once, long ago, a shepherd was out in the fields keeping watch over his flocks by night. At his side lay his leather bag with a sheepskin cloak inside and, close at hand, were his rod and staff in case of danger. Nearby, a fire burned brightly and three great savage dogs kept guard outside the flock as the sheep lay huddled so close together that there was no space between them. Now, the shepherd was a lonely man and because he was so unkind he had no friends.

As the night drew on, the shepherd became sleepy and his head began to nod. Suddenly, he was awakened by his dogs barking angrily. A stranger was coming towards him and the shepherd heard a voice saying, 'Kind friend, lend me some of your red coals from the fire. For my wife and her babe are in a cold cave that is used as a stable nearby and I must have a fire to warm her and the child.'

At once, the unkind shepherd called to his dogs. They crouched and sprang, but no sooner did they touch the stranger than they fell back and then, licked his hands as if he were a friend. Now the shepherd was angry, and seizing his staff he threw it at the stranger but, as it whizzed through the air, it suddenly turned aside and fell harmlessly to the ground. Then the stranger walked gently over the backs of the sheep and not one of them moved or was awakened.

'Kind friend,' he said again, 'Lend me some of your red coals from the fire. For my wife and her babe are in a cold cave that is used as a stable nearby and I must have a fire to warm her and the child.'

When the shepherd saw this man whom the dogs would not bite, nor a staff strike, he was afraid to refuse, but he thought, 'The fire is nearly out, and he has nothing in which to carry the red hot coals.'

The stranger stooped and gathered the glowing coals in his cloak and his hands were not burned neither was the cloak spoiled. Then the shepherd cried out, 'Who are you, whom dogs will not bite, nor staff strike, from whom sheep will not run and fire will not burn and, what night is this?'

'I cannot tell you,' answered the stranger. 'You will only believe if you see for yourself.'

So the shepherd arose and, taking his staff and leather bag, he followed the stranger who carried the burning coals. Over the hills they went until they came to a little town and there, in a stable, the shepherd saw a Mother with her babe.

Now the shepherd was an unkind man, but when he saw the Child lying there his heart grew kinder. Taking the soft sheepskin cloak from his leather bag, he gave it to the Mother, saying, 'Take this for the Child; for the night is cold.'

And no sooner had he done that one kind deed than his eyes were opened and he knew who the Strangers were. Suddenly, above his head he saw a host of angels praising God and saying, 'Glory to God in the highest and on earth peace, goodwill toward men.'

Then the shepherd knelt down in the stable and worshipped where the Baby Jesus lay sleeping in a manger.

Baboushka

It was the night the Christ Child came to Bethlehem. In a country far away from the manger, an old woman named Baboushka sat in her snug little house by a warm fire. The wind was drifting the snow outside and howling down the chimney, but it only made Baboushka's fire burn more brightly.

'How glad I am to stay indoors,' said Baboushka, holding her hands to the bright fire.

Suddenly she heard a knock on the door. She opened it and her candle shone on three men, dressed in fine clothes, standing outside in the snow. Their eyes shone kindly in the light of the candle and their arms were full of precious things.

'I am Melchior,' said the dark-skinned stranger, who carried a box of gold. 'We have travelled far, Baboushka, following a great star we have seen in the east. We stop to tell you of the Baby Prince born this night in Bethlehem and go to worship Him. Will you come with us?'

Baboushka shook her head, and the second stranger stepped forward, carrying sweet-smelling incense. 'I am Balthazar, King of Chaldea. We carry gifts to the Christ Child and go to worship Him. Will you come with us?'

Again, Baboushka shook her head and the third stranger spoke. He was fair of face and carried a box of precious ointment.

'I am Caspar,' he said. 'We stop to tell you of the Baby Prince born this night, who comes to rule the world and to bring goodwill to all men. Come with us, Baboushka, for we carry to Him precious gifts.'

But Baboushka looked at the driving snow and then inside at her cosy room and the crackling fire.

'It is too late for me to go with you, good sirs,' she said, 'and the weather is too cold.' She went inside and shut the door and, at once, the strangers turned and went on their way.

But as Baboushka sat by her fire, she began to think about the little Christ Child.

'Tomorrow I will go to find Him,' she said to herself, 'tomorrow when it is light I will take Him a gift of some toys.'

So, when it was morning, Baboushka put on her long cloak and filled a basket full of toys. Then, taking her staff, she set out to find the Christ Child.

But, alas, she had no star to guide her and had forgotten to ask the three strangers the way to Bethlehem. Try as she would, she could not catch them up for they had travelled too far along the road.

They say that old Baboushka is travelling still and, every Christmas Eve, when children are fast asleep, she knocks gently on the door, and leaves a toy from her basket for every child. Then, she hurries on through the years, forever in search of the little Christ Child.

The Christmas Rose

Once, in a cobbled street in Bethlehem, a little girl was playing. Her name was Joseel and she lived not far from an old inn. All day she had watched people coming and going along the street—rough shepherds from the fields and princes clad in robes of silk—all bearing presents to the stable by the inn. Often Joseel had tip-toed up to the stable door and peeped in to see the Infant Jesus lying in the manger. She liked to hear the doves cooing in the rafters and the cattle lowing in their stalls and to smell the warm scent of hay. But, above all, she longed to bring a gift like the others to give to Mary's Child.

But Joseel was only a little girl. Her parents were very poor and she had nothing to give, or money to buy a present. She had only empty hands to offer to the cradle of the Holy Babe.

Then a thought came into her mind. Outside the walls of Bethlehem, on the hills that surrounded the town, flowers grew. Joseel loved flowers and often wandered in the country picking the lilies that grew there. Yes, she would pick a bunch of flowers and offer them to the Baby Jesus.

Off she ran through the gates of the town and out into the country. Eagerly she searched the wayside but, alas, it was winter-time. Not a flower of any kind was to be found. All day she searched and, at last, tired and unhappy, Joseel walked homewards with tears in her eyes because she had found nothing that was worth offering to the Christ Child.

It was evening when she came again to Bethlehem and she ran through the dark streets to get home quickly. As Joseel passed the inn, she saw the golden glow of a lantern shining through the half-open stable door.

'I'll just peep in before I go home,' she whispered to herself and she tip-toed to the open door. Then she stopped, with a gasp of surprise, and took a step back. For there on the pathway, gleaming in the lantern light, grew a beautiful cluster of flowers. They had not been there that morning and they were a kind of flower that Joseel had never seen before.

'God must have planted them there,' she thought, 'for me to give to the Christ Child.' Carefully she gathered the beautiful white flowers and, holding them before her, ran joyfully into the stable with a present fit for a Baby King.

And that says the legend, is how Christmas Roses first came into the world.

The Twelve Months of the Year

Once, there was a girl called Anna who lived on the edge of a great forest. Anna was a sweet-tempered girl, but her stepmother and sister were very unkind to her. One New Year's Day, her sister Greta said, 'Go into the forest, Anna, and pick some violets for me to wear.'

Now Greta knew that there were no violets to be found in winter-time and, all that day, Anna searched the forest for them. By evening, she was cold and hungry and becoming frightened. Suddenly, she saw a fire among the trees and turned towards it. As she came nearer, she saw twelve blocks of stone and sitting on them were twelve strange beings. They were the Twelve Months of the Year.

'What brings you here?' said January in an icy voice and Anna told him she was looking for violets. 'Violets at this time of the year!' crackled January, 'they do not grow in the depth of winter.'

'I know,' said Anna, 'but my sister will be cross if I return home without them.'

January rose from his seat and gave his wand to the youngest of the months. 'Brother March,' he said, 'take the seat of honour.'

March obeyed and waved his wand over the fire. At once, the

flames leapt up to the sky, the snow disappeared and violets appeared among the green. Quickly, Anna gathered a bunch and thanking the Twelve Months she ran home as fast as she could.

Her stepmother and sister were amazed to see the violets, but they said nothing, not even thank you. The next day Greta said, 'Run into the forest and pick some strawberries,' and again poor Anna wandered into the dark forest looking, hopelessly, for strawberries in the snow. Then she saw the light of the fire and came again upon the Twelve Months.

'What brings you here?' said January, raising his white head.

'I'm searching for strawberries,' replied Anna, 'pray tell me where I can find them.'

January looked at June, who was opposite. 'Brother June,' he said, 'take the highest place.'

June obeyed and waved the wand. At once, the snow disappeared and star-shaped leaves quickly changed to ripe, plump strawberries and Anna was soon running home with her apron full of them. Her stepmother and sister were astonished, but they said nothing and ate all the strawberries, offering not one to Anna.

On the third day, Greta said, 'Anna, go into the forest and pick some nice red apples.' This time, Anna went at once to the Twelve Months as they sat by the fire.

'Red apples in winter?' said January. He looked at August who nodded towards September and the wand was handed over. As soon as September waved the wand, red apples appeared on the trees and joyfully Anna gathered them and took them home.

'Why didn't you gather some more?' shouted Greta, when Anna returned and, seizing her cloak, rushed into the forest to pick some more apples. Soon she came upon the Twelve Months.

'What do you seek?' said the great January.

'Mind your own business!' snapped Greta rudely, looking up at the trees.

Then January frowned and looked at December. Together they waved the wand and, at once, the sky became black with clouds and heavy snow began to fall. And, to this day, Anna and her stepmother are still waiting for Greta to return.

A Bible for Mary

There once was a little girl named Mary Jones, and she lived in a little village among the Welsh hills. Her mother and father were very poor, but even though their cottage was dark and cold, theirs was a happy home. Every week the family went to church, where

178

Mary heard the Bible stories read by the preacher, and on their way home Mary would talk about them. 'I wish I had a Bible,' she would say. And then, 'and I wish I could read.' But there was no one to teach Mary to read and, in those days, Bibles were very expensive. There were so few of them that only the rich could afford to buy one.

One day, a neighbour called on them and hearing that Mary could not read, she said, 'If you will learn to read, you may come up to the farmhouse and read in the Bible we have there.' But the days passed and the weeks, and the months and there was still no one to teach Mary how to read. She was quite a big girl when a school was started in the village, and Mary went every day. Soon she was reading. Mary worked very hard and, one evening, went proudly up to the farmhouse of the kindly neighbour and, to her great delight, read right through Psalm 23, 'The Lord is my shepherd'. Right through without a mistake.

But, now, Mary wanted the first part of her wish to come true—to own a Bible of her own. So, in the holidays, Mary worked to earn money. She ran errands, weeded the gardens, fetched and carried, minded babies—and she stored away the precious pennies that were given to her. So the time passed and the great day came when Mary found her money box full and heavy. She counted the coins carefully and found that she had enough to buy a Bible.

'Where can I get one?' she asked the neighbour.

'Well, there's a shop in the town of Bala. But that's twenty-five miles away.'

'I don't mind,' said Mary, and early one morning set off to walk to the town. On and on she plodded, and it was evening when she saw the lights of Bala flickering in the mist. It was too late to go to the shop, so she knocked at a house to ask for shelter for the night. They were kindly folk and gave her supper and a bed, and they promised to take her to the shop the next morning.

But when they got there, the shopkeeper shook his head. 'Sorry,' he said, 'I have only three Bibles left and they have been ordered. I'm afraid I cannot sell you one.' Mary was so disappointed that she burst out crying. She had worked and worked for nothing. She had tramped all those miles for nothing; she had waited all those years for nothing. There was no Bible for her.

But standing in the shop was a man who overheard what had happened. 'I have a Bible,' he said to Mary, 'here with me now. Take it.'

Mary, of course, went home delighted, but the man went home to think. And the result of his thinking was that he determined to form a Society so that poor people could get a Bible at a price they could

179

afford. And this was the beginning of the British and Foreign Bible Society—and you might say that it was because of Mary that millions of Bibles have been sent all over the world in more than a thousand languages.

Why the Owl is Cold

Once, long ago, there was a very cold winter. Deep snow lay over all the earth and long, shining icicles hung from the bare trees. King Frost had frozen and bitten off all the berries and the birds were very, very hungry.

Never had there been such a cold winter as this and the birds were so hungry that they gathered together to ask each other what was to be done. The first to speak was little Jenny Wren.

'The sun has been away for so long,' she said, 'that what we want is more fire on earth. If one of us was strong enough to fly to the sun and bring back new fire, then all might be well.'

Everyone agreed with Jenny Wren, but no one was brave enough to offer to fly on such a dangerous journey. They were all silent until Jenny Wren spoke again, 'As no one has offered,' she said, 'I will go.'

'But you will get burned by the great Sun,' cried the others.

'Yes, but I will bring back the fire,' replied Jenny Wren bravely.

What excitement there was when Jenny Wren took off for her long flight to the great Sun. Up and up she went above the trees, then into the clouds, when they could see her no more.

'We shall never see her again,' hooted the owl, who was always miserable.

'I hope we shall,' chirped the sparrow hopping about in the snow to keep himself warm.

Days went by and more days, and still Jenny Wren did not come back. The long winter went on and the birds were very cold and hungry. Then, one day, Jenny Wren flashed through the clouds carrying in her tiny claws a torch of flame. How they gathered round her to warm themselves with the bright blaze that she made with the fire from heaven! But, alas, when they looked at Jenny Wren they could hardly recognise her. The sun had scorched every feather from her body—all except her wings.

'Brave Jenny Wren,' they cried, 'to risk the great burning Sun for us. What can we do for you?'

Then up spoke Robin Redbreast. 'Let each one of us give her a feather,' he said, 'and she will be covered again.' No sooner had he said this than, one by one, the birds plucked a feather from their own bodies to give to Jenny Wren. Every bird—except the Owl.

'I am too-oo cold to spare a feather,' he hooted selfishly. 'Too-oo cold. Far too-oo cold.'

And, because he was so selfish, God the Father of them all was very displeased and this, the story says, is why the Owl has been cold ever since. And, because he would not spare one feather, he wears a ruff around his neck and he hoots in even the warmest weather.

The Shepherd with a Hundred Sheep

There was once a shepherd who had exactly a hundred sheep in his flock. There were old sheep and tiny baby lambs, black sheep and white sheep. It was a very large flock to care for, but the Shepherd was always patient and kind.

Every morning he led the flock over the mountain roads and beyond the hills to some green pasture where the sheep could feed on the rich grass. All day the sheep grazed, and drank from the brook, and lay under the shade of the olive trees. They had no fear, because the shepherd was always close by to watch over them.

Every evening, when the sky grew red with the sunset, he led them home again. He counted them as they went into the walled-in sleeping place called a fold. When he was quite sure that none was missing, he lit a fire outside the fold to frighten off the wild beasts which might be prowling near. Then he wrapped his cloak about him and lay down across the doorway, for the sheepfold had no door. Nothing could get by him to harm his sheep, for he, himself, was the door.

One evening, when thick black clouds covered the sky, the shepherd led his flock homeward through the cold wind and blinding rain. When he got to the fold, he stood at the doorway to count the sheep as they went in. 'One, two, three, four,' he counted and so on to 'ninety-seven, ninety-eight, ninety-nine'. And that was the last sheep.

'One is missing,' he said to himself. 'I must find the sheep that is lost, for it is alone somewhere in the mountains, frightened and in danger. I must go and find it.'

So he lit the fire and dragged branches of thorn across the doorway of the fold and, tired though he was, set off alone into the mountains.

The night was very dark. The rain beat down into his face and the stones and the thorns caught at his feet, but still he went on. There were no stars to light his way and he knew that wild beasts might be waiting in the darkness, but he climbed on over the rocks and stony ground calling the name of the lost sheep. Sometimes he stopped and listened for an answering 'baa-a,' but none came. Soon his hands were bruised and scratched and his legs could hardly carry him. But he did not even think of turning back. 'I will go on until I find it,' he said.

At last, when he had gone a long, long way, he found the lost sheep. It was so tired and frightened of scrambling up and down in the dark, that it was laying on a rocky ledge unable to move. The shepherd bent over it. He did not beat it or scold it. Gently, he lifted the sheep on to his shoulders and covering it with his warm cloak, he carried it home very glad and pleased.

Dawn was breaking as he came nearer to the houses of his friends and neighbours and he called to them as he went past. 'Rejoice with me,' he cried, 'I have found my lost sheep.' And that, said Jesus, is how God our Father cares for us.

St. Roche and his Little Dog

There was once a little dog and one sad day he was lost. He ran this way and that way looking for his home, but he only went further and further away. Soon, he was tired and hungry and his red tongue hung out with thirst. He ran up to passers-by and wagged his tail as if to say, 'Please take care of me; please give me a drink.' But no one took any notice of the little dog and he lay down panting in the dust.

Presently he pricked up his ears; someone was coming along the road and a man dressed in a pilgrim's robe came by. The little dog jumped up and ran to him, wagging his tail. The man stooped down and gave him a drink from his bottle and food from his wallet. Then he said, 'Poor old lost dog! Will you come with me?' And joyfully the little dog wagged his tail as they went off down the road together.

The man's name was Roche. He was a pilgrim, going from place to place helping anyone who was ill or in trouble. Presently he came to a great city, but the people in the streets were all hurrying to and fro with sad, unhappy faces and outside the houses people were lying on beds.

'What is the matter?' asked Roche of one of the passers-by.

'Many people are ill,' he answered. 'In every house someone is ill of a fever called the plague. We want to take them to hospital, but there are so many that there are not enough doctors and nurses to care for them and we have to lay them down in the streets.'

'I will go and help,' said Roche, and he and his little dog set off for the hospital.

When he came there he asked if he could help the sick people.

'Are you not afraid to catch the fever?' replied the doctors and nurses.

'No,' answered Roche, 'I am not afraid, for God will take care of me.'

So Roche stayed at the hospital and nursed the sick. He fed them and made them comfortable and, at night, he sat by them in the darkness so they would not feel lonely. All this time, his little dog lay quietly on the floor, but sometimes he jumped on to the beds and wagged his tail which made the sick people smile and forget their sadness.

But, one night, when Roche was in the hospital nursing the sick, he felt ill himself. He had caught the fever. 'I must not stay here,' he thought to himself, 'I will only give the doctors more work to do.' So calling his little dog, Roche crept out of the hospital and leaning heavily on his staff, he stumbled through the streets, past the city gates, and along the road into the country. His little dog followed, wondering why his master walked so slowly. At last, Roche came to a little wood where he lay down under the shady trees, unable to go any further. He could not remember what happened next, but he seemed to dream that God's angels were all about him and the trees bent down as if to comfort him. When he woke up, his little dog was standing by wagging his tail, and in his mouth was a loaf of bread. He had run to the woodman's cottage to get help and soon Roche heard footsteps and someone was bending over him. The woodman lifted Roche up in his strong arms and, taking him back to his cottage, nursed him back to health again. At last, Roche was quite well and set off on his journey again with his staff in his hand and his little dog by his side.

Paul, the Great Missionary

About five years after Jesus was born at Bethlehem another little boy, called Saul, was born in the city of Tarsus. When he grew up, he went to Jerusalem in order to become a priest. Now Saul was not a Christian. He hated the followers of Jesus, even to stoning them, and he asked that he might go to Damascus so that he could hurt the Christians who were there.

For many days he travelled and on the last day of the journey he saw the towers of Damascus in the distance. Then, suddenly, something wonderful happened. A great light from heaven shone round about him and Saul fell to the ground. Then he heard a voice saying to him, 'Saul, Saul, why do you persecute me?'

Trembling with fear, Saul said, 'Tell me, Lord, who are you?' and the voice replied, 'I am Jesus whom you are persecuting. But get up and go into the city, and you will be told what you have to do.'

Meanwhile, the men who were with Saul looked on speechless and frightened. They heard the voice but could see no one. When they lifted Saul from the ground they were more frightened than ever to discover that he was blind. They had to lead him by the hand for the last mile of the journey to Damascus, and he took no food or drink for three days.

One of the Christians in Damascus was a man named Ananias and Jesus spoke to him in a dream, saying, 'Go at once to Straight Street, to the house of Judas, and ask for a man from Tarsus named Saul. You will find him at prayer. He has had a vision of a man named Ananias coming in and laying his hands on him to restore his sight.'

At first, Ananias was afraid to go, for he knew that Saul had come to hurt the Christians, but the Lord said to him 'You must go, for this man is my chosen instrument to bring my name before the nations and their kings, and before the people of Israel. I myself will show him all that he must go through for my name's sake.'

So Ananias, because he loved Jesus, did as he was told and went to the house where Saul was. For three days Saul had been sitting there in his blindness. At last he heard the quiet footsteps of Ananias and he felt two hands gently touch his face and a voice said, 'Saul, my brother, the Lord Jesus, who appeared to you on your way here has sent me to you so that you may recover your sight, and be filled with the Holy Spirit.'

And, at once, Saul could see again and his strength returned. He was baptized by the followers of Jesus in Damascus, and he became a Christian. His name was changed to Paul and he became the great Christian missionary who took the teaching of Jesus to many nations.

The Greasy Cakes

It was a hot and dusty day, and in a village in China a little girl was playing just outside the open door of a cottage where she lived. Her name was Ah-leen and she was playing with her doll. At least, she called it her doll, but it was little more than a bundle of rags tied with straw. Ah-leen's father had died some years ago and there was little money to spare for toys. From the open door of the cottage came a lovely smell of cakes cooking. Her mother made these cakes to sell in the market-place. They were not the sort of cakes we have in this country—but the fatty, greasy cakes that the Chinese people love. They were really good cakes and Ah-Leen did not have much trouble selling them. Of course, she didn't get much money for them, but it was enough to keep them both alive. The little girl was glad to help her mother who managed to make the cakes, but was not well enough to stand in the market-place to sell them.

'Ah-Leen!' It was her mother's voice from inside the cottage, 'The cakes are ready now!'

Ah-Leen put down her doll and taking the cakes and her little tray set off for the market. Trade was good that day and, soon, Ah-Leen had sold all her cakes and the tray was empty. With her little bag jingling with coins she set off home. She hadn't far to go, and her heart was light as her bag was heavy. After walking for only a little while, she was stopped by a beggar.

'Spare a coin for a poor old man,' whined the beggar and Ah-Leen, who had a generous heart, opened her little bag of money. Suddenly, a hand shot out and the bag was torn from her grasp as the wretch made off with the lot. Poor Ah-Leen! She sat down by the roadside and wept as she thought of her mother who had worked so hard for nothing. As it happened, the chief man of the village came along the road that evening and, seeing the weeping girl, learned what had taken place.

'Weep not,' said he, 'we shall find the villain, wherever he is, and return the money.'

The police were called and a search was made. All along the roads and from house to house. But it was no use. The beggar had completely disappeared. So the Chief decided to try his own way. The village was not very big and he was the ruler of it, so he ordered that everyone was to pay a tax on a certain day, in the market-place, and he would watch to see that no one was missed. The day arrived and he sat in the market square and by his side was—a pail of water. One by one the people passed before him showing their money, then dropping it into the pail of water. This caused no surprise, for as many of them came in from the rice fields their hands were very grubby.

At last, a well dressed gentleman dropped his money in a haughty fashion. The coins sank to the bottom and the chief man watched. Then he cried out, 'Here is the thief! Guards seize him!' Everyone gasped, as no one had suspected this man. How did the chief man know? It was really quite simple. The cakes that Ah-Leen sold were oily and greasy and, in handling them, the little girl's money had become oily and greasy too. As the man dropped the coins into the water, the oil rose to the surface, and the thief was found out.

The Calling of Samuel

Once upon a time a baby was born in the land of Israel. His mother, Hannah, named him Samuel which means 'God-given' and, like all mothers, she hoped that one day he would grow up to be a good and great man among the people. In those days, to be a priest was to be very important, so when Samuel was old enough his mother took him to the Temple to be trained as a holy man.

The boy Samuel lived in the Temple and that was his home. He had many things to do such as running errands and carrying messages and getting the wood for the fire. He had to fill the lamps with yellow oil and, when darkness came, to light the floating wicks and set the lamps before the altar. He wore a small white tunic, called an ephod, which hung from his shoulders like a tiny gown and he learned to sing praises and to pray to God.

His master, whose named was Eli, was the High Priest and he was very old and almost blind. Samuel helped him in all the ways that a strong boy can help an old man. These were bad days in the land of Israel for God did not often speak to His people. But one night, after Eli had gone to lie down, God spoke to Samuel. The boy was laying down to sleep in the quiet shadows of the Temple curtains where the lamp of God was burning low. Then, in the stillness, he heard a Voice.

'Samuel!' called the Voice, 'Samuel!'

Thinking that it was Eli, the High Priest, Samuel jumped up and, on his bare feet, ran across to him.

'Here I am!' answered little Samuel, to the old man, 'you called me.'

But Eli was surprised to see him for he had said nothing. 'I did not call you,' said Eli. 'Lie down again.' So little Samuel went back to his mattress and lay down again.

Then a second time came the Voice, 'Samuel.' Again, Samuel jumped to his feet and ran to Eli.

'Here I am,' said the boy earnestly, 'for you did call me.'

But Eli shook his head. 'I did not call you. Lie down.'

So once more Samuel went back and lay down and all was quiet. Then, a third time, the silence was broken. 'Samuel,' said the Voice and again Samuel ran to Eli.

But this time Eli knew that the Lord had called to the child.

'Go and lie down,' he said to Samuel, 'and if you hear the Voice again, say "Speak Lord, for thy servant is listening".'

So Samuel lay down for the third time and listened. And the Voice came to him and Samuel answered as he had been told. Then

186

God told him that great changes were coming to the land of Israel, and that those who did wrong were to make way for those who did right. Then the Voice died away and all was quiet in the House of God. At first, Samuel was afraid to tell the High Priest for it was Eli's sons who had done the greatest wrong. But then Samuel did tell him, keeping nothing back.

'This comes from the Lord,' said Eli, 'His will be done.'

The Gift of Light

Once, long ago, there lived a king who had two sons. As he looked at the two princes, so straight and tall, he wondered which of the two would be the best to rule the kingdom when he was gone. Both were strong and skilled with the sword, both could shoot an arrow to its mark and ride the swiftest horse, and the king could not make up his mind. 'The one to be chosen,' thought the king to himself, 'must not only be brave and strong. He must be wise as well as good.' So he decided to set them a test.

One evening, when the day's work was done, he called the two boys to his side and said to them, 'The hour is late, my sons, but early tomorrow morning, before sunrise, I want you to go into the market place and buy me something that will fill the whole of my house.' And into the hand of each boy he placed one small copper coin. 'It is a test,' he said, 'to find out which of you is the wiser and fit to rule my kingdom when I am gone.' And with that, he bade them both good-night.

As each boy looked at the small coin in his hand, they wondered how they were going to buy enough to fill the whole house but, not wishing to displease their father, they rose very early in the morning and made their way to the market place. Then, each one went his own way through the stalls and loaded wagons and people buying and selling—even at that early hour.

'Now what can I buy with my copper coin,' said the first boy as he went from stall to stall. 'Rice, perhaps?' But no, he had only one small copper coin and that was not enough to buy one sackful. 'Ripe fruit from the orchards?' That was too expensive. 'Dried fish, bags of sugar, spices and salt, bales of cotton?' As he searched from stall to stall he knew that the one small copper coin would not buy nearly enough to fill his father's house. All day he searched the market place and the long shadows began to fall as evening was coming on. At last, he came to a stall stacked high with bales of yellow straw.

'That is cheap and light to carry,' he said to himself. 'I will buy straw.' So he struck a bargain with the stall-keeper and bought as much straw as he could carry with his one small copper coin. But when he got back that evening, the straw was not nearly enough to fill his father's house. Try as he could, it covered only the floor of one room.

Then, when it was quite dark, his brother returned. He, too, had searched the long, long day with one copper coin for something that would fill his father's house. And when, the king saw his gift he was very pleased. 'You are the wise son!' he said, 'you have shown true wisdom and are fit to have the kingdom that I will leave!'

For the second son, with his one small copper coin, had bought tiny candles and when they were lit and set on stands, they shone through the darkness and filled the whole of his father's house with light.

Martin, the Cobbler

Martin, the shoemaker, lived in a poor little room with one window which looked out on to a cobbled street. Every morning he would sit by the window and mend shoes. He always had plenty of shoes to mend because he worked carefully and used only the best leather. When evening came, Martin would light the lamp and take down his Bible to read again the stories of the Gospel. As he read the story of the poor welcome that the rich man gave to Jesus, Martin said to himself, 'If Jesus came to my house, would I welcome him like that?' Thinking over the story, he pillowed his head on his arms and presently fell asleep. Suddenly he heard a voice calling him. 'Martin! Martin! Keep watch in the street, for tomorrow I shall come!'

Martin sat up and rubbed his eyes and looked around his little room. But there was no one there so, thinking that he must have been dreaming, he went to bed.

The next morning he was up early. He lit the fire and made some tea and, going to the window, he set to work mending shoes. Had he really heard the voice of Jesus last night? The snow lay thick on the cobbles in the street outside and presently an old man came along sweeping it away. Martin could see how weak and cold the old man was and he beckoned him in. Together they sat drinking the hot tea and the old man gratefully stretched his frozen hands towards the fire.

'Are you expecting anyone?' said the old man, seeing that Martin kept looking through the window.

'Perhaps,' replied Martin and he told him of his dream.

A little while later the old man, feeling much better, left and Martin settled down to work again.

Presently he saw a mother carrying her little child. Dressed in rags, she was shivering with the cold and the baby was crying for she had no shawl to keep him warm.

'Come in here,' called Martin and the woman gladly obeyed. He sat her by the fire and gave her a drink of hot soup then, finding an old cloak, he wrapped it round the woman and child and set them on their way.

Still Martin watched, but it was now late afternoon and Jesus had not come. Then he saw a woman with a heavy basket of apples. As she put it down to rest awhile, a ragged little boy ran up behind her and snatched an apple from the basket, but the woman turned and caught him. Angrily she seized his hair and began to beat him. Martin ran out into the street.

'Forgive him,' he said, 'I will pay for the apple.'

He spoke to them and the woman softened. The boy, ashamed and sorry, helped the woman to carry her heavy basket.

That night, Martin lit his lamp and picked up his Bible. Then his dream came back to him and from the shadows there came a voice.

'Martin! Martin! Don't you know me?'

'Who is it?' asked Martin.

'It is I,' said a voice and from the shadows stepped the old man with his spade. Then he vanished and again a voice said, 'It is I,' and the woman and her baby came from the shadows and they, too, vanished. 'It is I,' and out of the darkness stepped the old apple-woman and the boy, smiling. And they, too, disappeared.

Then Martin glanced at his open Bible and read these words. 'For when I was hungry, you gave me food; when thirsty you gave me drink. When I was a stranger you took me into your home . . . anything you did for one of my brothers here, however humble, you did for me.'

Martin then knew that his dream had come true and that he had welcomed Jesus into his house that day.

The Juggler in the Monastery

Once upon a time, many years ago, there lived a juggler who was well known in the towns and villages of France. Every summer he travelled the dusty roads, doing his tricks for a few pence. He carried a worn square of carpet, some knives and plates, and six shining balls, and when he came to a village he would put down his square of carpet and begin his performance. His jokes were not very good and his juggling was not very skilful, but he never failed to get a clap when he finished his act by throwing into the air at one time the

189

six shining balls. Afterwards he would bow to the crowd, gather their coins in his shabby hat, and go on to the next village.

So it went on; but he never made enough money to keep himself through the long winter months. His body was thin and his clothes were ragged and often he slept by the roadside. It was not surprising that one bitterly cold winter's morning he fainted and was found lying in a ditch by a monk. The monk lifted the juggler into his strong arms and carried him, as if he had been a babe, to the monastery.

There the juggler was cared for and shown much kindness. Days became weeks and weeks became months and the juggler became strong again and was ready to take to the roads. But one thing troubled him. He had no way of making a thankoffering to God in the monastery church.

The monks were able to sing and chant and he knew no hymns or psalms. The monks could make beautiful Bibles and stained glass windows but the juggler could not do that. But there was one thing he could do. He could offer his skill at juggling.

So one evening, in the darkened church, he tiptoed down the long aisle and laid his threadbare piece of carpet before the altar. And there the juggler, who was truly thankful, went through all his tricks; spinning the plates and throwing the knives and the six shining balls to the best of his ability.

As it happened, one of the monks came into the church and saw what was happening. Horrified at what he had seen, the monk ran to find the Abbot who was the head of the monastery.

'Come quickly,' he gasped, 'that foolish juggler is spoiling our church. He is doing his stupid tricks on holy ground before the altar.'

And, together, they rushed to the church.

The Abbot was speechless with anger. But as he ran forward to drag the juggler away, the darkened church was suddenly ablaze with light which shone around the juggler as he knelt on his worn carpet to receive the blessing. All the prayers and praises of the monks, all their hymns and psalms had never received a blessing such as this, and the Abbot and his monks stole quietly away.

The humble thankoffering of the grateful juggler had been accepted.

St. Valentine and the Blind Girl

In the great city of Rome there once lived a little girl who was blind. There were beautiful buildings and sunny streets in the city, but the little girl could not see the marble buildings nor the sunny streets. She could only feel the hot sun and hear footsteps of the passers-by. No one had ever told her the Christmas Story or taught

190

her the Lord's Prayer. But one day she came to know—and this was how it happened.

The little girl's father was a judge called Asternis and his lord was the Roman Emperor who was King over the city. One day, Asternis was called before the great Roman Emperor. The Emperor was sitting on his throne, guarded by his soldiers, and before him stood a prisoner bound in chains. The prisoner was Valentine, who was a Christian and one of the great followers of the Lord Jesus.

As Asternis came before the throne, the Emperor spoke to him. 'Take this man Valentine,' he said, 'and keep him as a prisoner in your house. Put him under lock and key for he is a Christian and will not give up speaking of Jesus Christ.'

Asternis bowed to the Emperor and then he took Valentine out of the palace and through the sunny streets of Rome until they came to his house.

The little blind girl was waiting for her father as she always did. She knew the sound of his step but she waited for she could hear that a stranger was with him. Then she heard the stranger say, 'Bless everyone in this house and help them to know Jesus Christ who is the Light of all the world.'

The little girl had never heard the name of Jesus before and she wondered about whom the stranger could be speaking. Then she heard her father say, 'Why do you say Jesus Christ, the Light of all the world?'

'Because,' said Valentine, 'it is Jesus Christ who brings light and happiness to everyone.'

Then the little girl's father replied, 'If this be true as you say, I will put it to the test. I have a little daughter who is blind. If you can restore her sight I will believe that Jesus is the Light of all the world and I will become a follower of your Master.'

The little girl heard her father call, 'Come, little daughter.'

So she stretched out her hands to feel her way towards him. As she came nearer, she heard the voice of Valentine say, 'Lord Jesus Christ, who art the True Light, give light to this Thy child.'

And, at once, the little girl opened her eyes and could see the sunshine and the blue sky and the great house where she lived.

And everyone in that great house on that day became Christian and rejoiced with St. Valentine who followed Jesus to the end.

The Dog Brother

One day, long ago, a slave escaped from his cruel master. He slipped away when no one was looking and, as soon as he reached the open country, he ran as fast as he could through the mountains, for if he was caught he would be put to death. That was the punishment. On and on he ran, panting and gasping for breath, stopping sometimes to listen for anyone following, and then stumbling on alone over the stony, mountain pathway. Once he stopped and, when he put his ear to the ground, he could hear the sound of many men hunting for him. He sprang to his feet and ran on, even faster, and soon came to an empty and deserted village. Panting, the slave stopped and looked for a hiding place. At last, he found the very place—just a hole in the ground—and carefully he dropped into it.

It was deeper than he thought and he fell a long way but, luckily, he was unhurt. He found that it was an old, dried-up well and, as he crouched at the bottom, he heard the sound of men above looking for him. Through the village they went, but no one thought of looking down the well and soon the sound of their footsteps faded away.

'Now,' thought the slave, 'I will climb out and escape,' and he began to climb the side of the well. Again and again he tried, only to fall back again, for it was far too steep. As he looked up at the small circle of sky far above him, he realised that he was again a prisoner.

Many hours passed by. The circle of sky grew dark and then, as night passed, began to grow light again. Then he heard a scuffling sound and, looking up, he saw a dog looking down at him. The slave called, but the dog went away. Hours passed again, and this time he was more lonely than before. Then the dog returned and he saw that it was carrying some meat in its mouth which it dropped down the well. The slave ate it hungrily, for he was starving, and he felt much better. After that, the dog came often to the well with food.

But, not far away, in the monastery of the Brothers of St. John, they noticed that one of their dogs, although fed regularly, was looking thin and hungry. So they put down more food and stood watching from a distance. The dog picked up the food and trotted through the gate and out of the monastery, and the Brothers followed. Soon they came to the well where the slave was a prisoner and the Brothers hauled him out. Taking him back to the monastery, they nursed the slave back to health and gave him his freedom once more, for the Brothers of St. John, like the Good Samaritan of old, knew well the words, 'Thou shalt love thy neighbour as thyself.'

The Silver Candlesticks

Jean Valjean was a woodchopper's son and when he was very young his father and mother died. His older sister took care of him with her own large family, but they were very poor and there was never enough to eat.

One winter, when they were without food and the children were crying with hunger, Jean stole a loaf of bread. He was caught and sent to prison for five years where he was chained with an iron collar round his neck. Several times he tried to escape but each time he was caught and more years were added to his sentence. As a result, he was in prison for nineteen years for stealing one loaf of bread.

When, at last, he left the prison he had nowhere to go and all doors were closed against him. No inn would give him shelter and no home would give him welcome. Finally, he went to the house of a good Bishop, who was a kindly man and loved by everyone.

'See here,' he said, when the door was opened to his knock, 'my name is Jean Valjean and I have been a prisoner for nineteen years. No one will give me shelter and I am tired and hungry.'

'Come in,' said the kindly Bishop, 'warm yourself by the fire and you will take supper with me tonight and sleep here.'

That night Jean slept in a bed for the first time for twenty years. He had been a peaceful man but now, as he lay in the darkness, the thought of all the unkindness and cruelty he had suffered came into his mind and he decided to have his revenge. Quietly he crept downstairs and taking all the silver he could find he put it into a basket and, escaping through the garden, he fled into the dark night.

Some hours later, Jean Valjean was brought back to the Bishop's house by three police guards. 'We caught him running away with a basket full of silver,' they said.

'Oh, you are back again!' said the Bishop to Jean Valjean. 'I am glad to see you. But you forgot the candlesticks when you left. Here, take them.' And he gave some silver candlesticks to Jean.

'So you gave him the silver?' said the police. 'We thought he was a thief.'

'Let him go,' said the Bishop. 'The silver is his as a gift from me.'

'Is it true,' whispered Jean Valjean to the Bishop, 'that I am free and can go?'

'Yes,' the Bishop replied, 'but go through the front door which is always open to you day and night. And remember that you have promised to use the money to become an honest man.'

Jean did not remember promising anything, but, the Bishop went on, 'You no longer belong to evil but to good. I have bought your soul for you and given it to God.'

From that time onward Jean Valjean remembered the forgiveness of the kindly Bishop and became a different man. And he kept those silver candlesticks to remind him until the end of his days.

John the Baptist

When Jesus was growing up in Nazareth, there lived a boy named John who was His cousin. As John grew up, he could see the cruelty of the Roman soldiers and the greediness of the Jews around him, and he longed for the day when a Leader would come to show them the right way to live.

So when John became a man, he said goodbye to his mother and father and he went into the wilderness to think and to pray. The wilderness is the wild, empty land west of the Dead Sea. John had no money and he did not want any. The only clothes he wore were a long cloak of camel's hair and a leather belt around his waist, and he ate the food of the very poor—insects called locusts and honey from the wild bees.

Then, one day, John came out of the wilderness to the banks of the River Jordan to tell people that they must make ready for the great Leader who was to come.

'What shall we do?' the people asked, and John told them not to be selfish and proud but to help one another. Then the soldiers asked what they ought to do, and John replied, 'Be gentle and just with the people, and be content with the money you earn.'

Crowds of people came to John to be baptised by him and, because of this, he was known as John the Baptist. They became very excited because they thought that John was the great Leader, or Messiah, but he said to them, 'There is someone coming who is greater than I, whose shoes I am not fit to unfasten.'

One day, Jesus arrived from Galilee and He went to the banks of the River Jordan. John saw Him coming and said, 'Behold, the Lamb of God!' and to John's amazement, Jesus stepped down into the water to be baptised.

At first, John refused, saying, 'I need to be baptised by you—yet you come to me.' But Jesus quietly replied, 'Let it be so, for only in this way can we follow the will of God.'

Then John baptised Jesus in the waters of the River Jordan and, as he did so, it seemed to him that the Spirit of God descended like a dove and he heard a voice saying, 'This is my beloved Son, in whom I am well pleased.'

This wonderful happening on the banks of the River Jordan marks the beginning of the work of Jesus. But, first, He went away into the wilderness and stayed there for forty days, hungry and alone, to prepare Himself for the great work that was to come.

It is in this season of Lent that we remember the forty days that Jesus went without food in the wilderness after He was baptised by John the Baptist.

The Legend of the Woodpecker

There was once a little old woman who lived all alone in a cottage in the woods. Her name was Gerda and she always wore a shiny black dress, a red bonnet on the back of her head, and a big white apron tied with a bow. Because she lived all alone and thought of no one but herself, Gerda had become very selfish. For years she had never given away a present or invited anyone in for a cup of tea.

One day, a man was journeying through the woods. He had come a long way and was very tired and hungry. Just as he felt he could go no further, he spied Gerda's cottage through the trees. Weary and faint from the lack of food he made his way towards it and knocked on the door.

'Who can that be?' said Gerda angrily and, leaving the oven where she was baking some cakes, she opened the door.

'Can you spare some food?' said the man as the door was opened, 'for I have travelled far and am faint from hunger. I have no money to pay you, but whatever you wish for, that you shall have.' Gerda almost slammed the door in his face for she was very mean and hated giving anything away.

But, with very bad grace, she went to the oven and taking up a small lump of dough placed it inside. To her surprise, when the cake was cooked, it covered the plate.

'That's too much to give away,' she muttered to herself and, taking an even smaller piece of dough she baked a second cake. That, too, when cooked was as large as ever. Gerda, by this time, was really angry and taking the tiniest scrap of dough the size of a button she tried again. The cake, when cooked, was still as large as ever.

'You must go without,' said Gerda to the hungry man. 'All that I cook is too big for the likes of you!' and she shut the oven door with a bang.

When the poor man was gone, Gerda began to feel sorry for her meanness.

'I wish I were a bird,' she said, 'then I could fly to that hungry man with the largest cake on the shelf.'

And, all at once, the little old woman began to grow smaller and smaller. Her nose changed to a beak, her arms stretched out until they were wings, and she flew away up the chimney and into the woods among the trees.

If you look, you may see her today. She still wears her shiny black dress, her white apron, and the red bonnet on the back of her head. But all day long she must run up and down the trunks of the trees, pecking on the hard bark in search of food. And if you listen carefully in the month of February, you will hear her tap, tap,

195

tapping away, for the selfish old woman was changed into a red-headed wood-pecker.

St. David and the Robbers

Long ago, in a valley in Wales, a boy was born who became the patron saint of that country. His name was David and he grew up strong and healthy, loving to be out in the country or listening to the Bible stories his mother told him. Like David in the Bible this Welsh boy was tall and straight and he had a sweet voice for singing the Psalms.

David loved God very much and he wanted to tell other people about Him too so, when he was old enough, he went to study and work in a big church called a monastery. When he had learned as much as he could, David made up his mind to build a monastery himself where he could teach men to spread the Good News of Jesus to all the people of Wales. He chose a place not far from his house and, with his friends, he began to build.

But, not far from where David began his building, there lived a powerful robber named Boia, who soon came around to see what was going on. He found David's friends busy at their work of digging the earth and clearing the ground, carrying stones and cutting down trees. Now Boia knew that with these holy men nearby, he could no longer go on robbing and stealing so, with great cunning, he said to them, 'Why do you work at this hard life of digging and carrying heavy stones. Why not join me and live at ease?'

But David's men were not to be won over and said that they would rather work honestly than live by stealing.

'You talk like fools,' said Boia and he went away very angry.

When the robber chief returned home and his wife heard that he had failed to stop David's men from building the monastery, she said, 'We must stop these monks from building their church. We will spoil their work so that they will be driven away.'

During the next few days, David and his men found that their work was much harder. Logs of wood made ready for building had been rolled away during the night. Stones placed in position were tumbled over by the next morning and rocks and boulders were thrown back on to the place from where they had been cleared.

But nothing could stop David and his men. Cheerfully they worked all the harder and, in good time, the monastery was finished and the robber chief left that valley for ever.

As time went on, David's fame spread far and wide throughout the country. Many stories are told of the wonders he worked

196

and years later, as St. David, he was made the patron saint of Wales.

The Wind and the Sun

Once upon a time the Wind and the Sun had a quarrel. They were always arguing with one another for the Wind was rather jealous of the Sun. Everybody could see the Sun in the sky but you could never see the Wind—only the things he moved by his strength. One day they met on a hill and began to boast of the wonderful things that they could do.

'I,' cried the Sun, 'am able to bring the summer to ripen the fruits and wheat and cover the earth with flowers.'

'And I,' sighed the Wind, 'can break the trees and move the seas and bring the winter.'

So they quarrelled, and each ended where he had begun, thinking that he had the greater power.

'Anyway,' said the Wind to the Sun, 'I am stronger than you are.'

The Sun beamed with a broad smile: 'We shall soon see about that,' he replied.

Just then they saw a man walking up the hill wearing a thick overcoat.

'As I am stronger than you are,' said the Wind, 'let us put it to the test. Being stronger, I can take off that man's coat before you can.'

'Try,' said the Sun, and he hid behind a cloud while the Wind began to blow as hard as he could upon the man. With all his strength he puffed and puffed but the harder he blew the more closely the man wrapped his coat about him. The trees bent and the leaves swirled as the Wind howled down the hill, but the man only buttoned his coat more tightly and bent his head as he walked along. Try as he would the Wind could not remove the man's coat and he gave up in despair.

'Now let me try,' beamed the Sun as he came out from behind the cloud.

Gently the Sun began to shine and, as he felt a little warmer, the man unbuttoned his coat collar. The Sun shone hotter still and the man, feeling warmer and warmer, threw open his coat as he climbed the hill. Then the Sun sent his hottest rays right down upon the man's head. The heat became too much for the man and he threw off his coat and made for the woods, where he lay down to cool off in the shade of the trees.

'Do you still think you are stronger, Mr. Wind?' asked the Sun, but, by this time, the Wind was a gentle breeze as he blew himself away to the south never to argue with the Sun again.

197

Two Stories

Here are two stories that show the love and care that mothers have for their children. The first story comes from Scotland.

Some years ago, some workmen were cutting rock from a quarry. To do this they would bore a hole in the rock, fill it with gunpowder, attach a fuse and, when all was ready, give the alarm and go back to a safe distance. The explosion would blow tons of rock into pieces. One day the unexpected happened. The fuse was alight, the workmen had gone back to a safe distance, and they were waiting for the explosion. Suddenly a child of about three began to wander across the open space towards the quarry.

Every second death was rushing on him. The workmen did the only thing they could think of, calling to him, shouting and waving their arms, but the child only stood looking at them, not understanding what they meant. No man dare run forward, for the explosion was about to happen and though they shouted loudly the child never thought of moving. Rescue came only just in time.

The child would have been killed had not his mother appeared. She understood at once and did the one thing a mother would do in time of danger. To have run towards the child might have sent him running nearer the quarry. To have called might have frightened him. What she did was to kneel down and open her arms. At once, the child ran towards her and when the air shook with the explosion he was safe.

The second story comes from London. Peter's father kept a shop and Peter was a very useful little boy. On Saturday morning he used to clean the knives and forks, polish the shoes, do his mother's shopping, and help in his father's shop. At dinner-time he always saw a bright new sixpence shining at him from the centre of his white plate. But one Saturday his mother quite forgot the precious sixpence, so on Sunday morning at breakfast time she saw a note on her plate. Peter had taken one of his father's shop bills and had written this on it: Owing to Peter from his mother. For cleaning knives and forks—2d.: For polishing shoes—1d.: For helping in the shop—3d.: total 6d.

Peter's mother read the bill but never said a word. On Monday morning, Peter had a note on his plate. This is what it said: Owing to Mother from Peter: For washing, feeding and clothing Peter for four years, when a baby—Nothing: For nursing Peter during six weeks illness—Nothing: For holidays by the sea, parties at Christmas, presents and toys and books for ten years—Nothing: Total—Nothing.

Peter read the note and understood.

The Christian Fire

Hundreds of years ago, on a farm near the coast, there lived a boy named Patrick. When he was about 16 years old, some pirates landed on the shore near his home, stealing cattle and seizing prisoners. Patrick was carried off to Ireland, where he was sold as a slave and sent into the lonely mountains to feed pigs.

One night, Patrick escaped. He had two hundred miles to go to reach the coast, travelling only at night time in case he was caught. At last he reached the coast and found a ship ready to sail, but the captain refused to take him. So Patrick went back to the shore and prayed for help and he seemed to hear a voice saying, 'Go back, for the men are calling you.'

Patrick hurried back to the ship and was overjoyed when the captain said, 'Come, the crew have found a place for you.'

The ship set sail and, after three days, they reached the coast of Brittany. Here, Patrick set off on a dangerous journey through the forests until he came to a monastery on a river bank, where he found shelter. For three years he lived there, learning all he could to become a holy man, but Patrick knew he must return to Ireland to spread the Good News of Jesus, so again he set off for the wild Irish coast with a band of monks.

When Patrick and his friends landed, the people thought they were pirates and ran to tell the chieftain, who came ready to fight them. But, instead of pirates, the chieftain found unarmed and friendly strangers. 'Put down your weapons,' he cried to his followers, 'these men are friends not enemies.'

The chieftain listened to all Patrick had to say and, after some time, he was baptised and became a Christian. He gave his barn to Patrick as a home, which became the first church in Ireland.

But the power of the heathen Druids was still very strong, and at Easter-time they held a great spring festival. All fires had to be put out, on pain of death, and then they lit a huge fire on a hill to drive away the winter god. Now Patrick wanted to show them all that at Easter-time they should worship Jesus, not a heathen god, so he went to another hill ten miles away. There he prepared a fire and, suddenly, in the darkness he lit the Sacred Flame and a blaze of light shot up from the hill.

The King and the heathen Druids were amazed to see the strange flames when all should have been in darkness. In haste they went towards the fire and would have killed Patrick, but he showed no fear.

'Who are you and what is your errand here?' demanded the King.

199

'I am a torch-bearer,' replied Patrick. 'I bring the true light to lighten this dark land and to spread peace and goodwill.'

Because Patrick showed such courage and in spite of the anger of the heathen Druids, the Irish King listened and Patrick was allowed to spread the message of Jesus throughout the land and many people became Christians. The light from St. Patrick's fire had quenched the fire of the heathens for ever.

The Angel of the Flowers

Long, long ago, when God first made the world, the Angel of the Flowers came down on earth and wandered in field, and forest, and garden, to find the flower she liked the best of all. As she wandered in her search, she came upon a gay tulip, all yellow and red, standing tall and proud in a garden, and the Angel said to the tulip, 'Where would you like to live most of all?'

'I would like to live on a castle lawn in the velvety grass,' said the tulip, 'where my lovely colours would show up against the grey, castle walls and everyone would see how beautiful I am.'

Sadly, the Angel turned away from the proud and boastful tulip and spoke to the rose.

'Where would you like to stay most of all?' she asked the rose.

'I would like to climb the castle walls,' said the rose, 'for I am weak and frail and not able to climb myself. I need help and shelter.'

The Angel of the Flowers turned sadly away from the rose and wandered on until she came to the violet growing in the dark forest, and she said to the violet, 'Where would you like to live most of all?'

'Here, in the forest, where I am hidden from everyone,' said the violet. 'No one can pluck me; the brook cools my feet and the trees stop the sun from spoiling my beautiful colour.'

But the Angel turned away from the violet and went on until she came to the sturdy, yellow dandelion growing in the meadow grass.

'And where would you like to live most of all?' said the Angel to the dandelion.

'Oh,' cried the dandelion, 'I would like to live wherever happy children can find me when they run to school or romp and play in the fields. I want to live by the roadside, and in the fields, and grow between the stones in the back yards and make every one glad because of my bright colour.'

'You are the flower I like most of all,' said the Angel of the Flowers, as she laid her hand upon the dandelion's curly, yellow head. 'You shall blossom from spring till autumn and be the children's flower.'

And that is why the dandelion comes so early and pushes her head up everywhere—by hedge and field, and house and wall, and has such a long, sweet life.

The Song in the Night

It was evening and the great hall was lit by flaring torches. The meal was finished and, at one end of the long table, a man took up a harp and began to play. As he played he sang and when he had finished he passed the harp to the one sitting next to him. This man, too, had a song and struck a merry tune upon the strings. Then the harp was passed to the next and the next, for this was long ago when almost everyone could make music to while away the long winter evenings.

But one man was unhappy. He watched the harp coming nearer as he sat next to the door of the great hall. 'It will be my turn soon,' he thought, 'they will ask me to play and sing and I can do neither. I'll slip away when no one is looking.' So, after the next song during the noise of the clapping, Caedmon rose quietly from the table and went out into the night.

It was cold and dark after the warmth and firelight of the hall and Caedmon crossed the courtyard to the stables where he slept. He was a cowhand and the animals were in his care. Moving gently, he went to each one to see that they were comfortable and then lay down on some straw, for this was his only bed. In the darkness he thought of the warm and cheery hall and longed to be there, singing with the others. He thought of the Church where he heard even better singing, but the Church hymns were written in Latin and Caedmon, the poor cowhand, could not even understand them, let alone join in. Thinking about these things, he fell asleep. Then came a voice.

'Caedmon! Caedmon!' He sat up. Out of the darkness of the stable there was someone standing bathed in light and Caedmon knew that he was looking at an angel. 'Caedmon, sing me a song.'

'I cannot sing,' stammered Caedmon, 'I left the hall tonight because I cannot sing.'

'But you shall sing to me,' was the reply.

With wonder Caedmon replied, 'What shall I sing?'

'Sing about the beginning of the world when God made a garden,' said the Angel, and Caedmon began to sing. He loved that story in the Bible and he began to make up a song about the earth and the sky, and trees and the birds. His voice rose in that dark stable, a voice singing in English that everyone could understand.

Next morning, when Caedmon awoke, the song was still ringing

201

in his head. 'I must have been dreaming,' he thought. 'But dream or not, I must tell someone.' So he went to the chief one, called Mother Hilda.

'I have never been able to sing,' he said to her, 'but last night . . .' and he explained what had happened.

'Sing this song to me,' she replied gently, and Caedmon sang again the song in the night.

'My son,' she said, 'God has give you this gift. It must not be lost. You cannot read the Bible because it is in Latin, but the stories must be read to you in English so that you can turn them into song.'

Every day, after that, Caedmon would listen as the Bible stories were explained to him and then he would make them into songs— the first of our hymns.

St. Cuthbert and the Eagle

One evening, many years ago, a man and a boy were walking through the high hills and mountains of Scotland. The boy's name was Cedda and he was bringing a holy man, called St. Cuthbert, to his village to tell them about God. The hour was late and, as the darkness grew, the rain began to fall.

'How far is it to your village?' asked St. Cuthbert.

'Many miles, master,' quavered the boy, for in the gloom he had mistaken the footpath and was now hopelessly lost.

'Perhaps we shall soon find food and shelter,' replied St. Cuthbert.

'Alas,' replied the boy, who was now very hungry and frightened, 'no one lives in these wild parts.'

'Take heart,' said the holy man, 'and pray to God to send us help.' So they prayed and then journeyed on.

Suddenly, above them as they walked, they heard the whirr of wings and, looking up, saw a great bird called an eagle swooping down to earth. Down, down it came to a river which ran at the foot of the hills where they were walking.

'Run and see what he has caught,' said St. Cuthbert, 'perhaps God has answered our prayer.'

The boy scrambled down the hill to where the river swirled over the rocks and he found the eagle with its talons fastened upon a large salmon which it had caught. The eagle's wings were beating as it tried to rise with its prey, but the fish was too big and heavy. As the boy came nearer, the eagle dropped the fish and flew off a little way and wheeled above him, staring with red and angry eyes.

'Here is our supper!' called Cedda.

'Wait,' said St. Cuthbert, 'God has sent the eagle. We must not forget that His creatures can be hungry, too.'

So they divided the fish and placed a large piece on a stone by the river. The great eagle swooped down and, seizing it, flew off high up into the sky.

As they sat down to cook and eat the food, Cedda suddenly called out. 'Why, master, here is the path by the river that leads to my village. It is the one I missed many miles back.'

St. Cuthbert smiled, 'God has indeed answered our prayers,' was all he said.

Brand of Iceland

Long, long ago, in a country of snow and hot springs called Iceland, there lived a man named Brand. One day, taking his long boat with a square sail, he sailed across the stormy sea to the land of Norway. Now, Brand was a very good man, kind and generous to all who knew him, and the King of Norway, hearing of his kindness and knowing that he was in the country, decided to test him.

As he was the King, he called to him a friend of Brand and said to him, 'They tell me that Brand is a very kind man who will give to rich and poor and to all who come begging at his door. Go and ask him for the cloak he is wearing.' It was winter time in Norway and very cold and the King knew that this was a hard test.

The friend left the King and went to Brand, where he found him working on his boat. Brand was wearing a scarlet jacket and, across his shoulders, a cloak of the same colour hemmed with gold. As he was a Viking, an axe hung from his wrist but this had a golden handle.

'The King would have your cloak,' said the friend.

At once, without word or question, Brand slipped the cloak from his shoulders and gave it to him, and the man returned with it to the King.

The King was very surprised. 'He is very kind and generous,' he said, 'but let us test him further. Go back and ask him for his axe.'

The King knew that a Viking prized his axe above all things and thought that this would be a severe test.

Again, the friend returned to Brand. 'The King would have your axe,' he said.

At once, without a word or a question, Brand slipped the axe with the golden handle from his wrist and gave it to him, and the man returned with it to the King.

The King was very pleased, but also puzzled. 'He is, indeed, very

203

kind and more generous than any man I know. But there must be a limit to what he will give away. Go back and ask him for his jacket.'

Brand's friend did not want to do this but, because it was the King, he returned yet again and did as he was commanded. 'The King would have your jacket.' Without a word or a question, Brand handed over the garment but, this time, he took out his sword and cut off one sleeve of the jacket, and the man returned with it to the King.

When the King saw this, he smiled, 'This man is not only kind and generous, but he is wise, too. By this jacket with one sleeve, he has told me that I am like a man with one hand, always taking, never giving. Bid him to come to me and I will show him the other hand by returning to him precious gifts and great honour.'

So Brand went to live in the King's palace and was greatly honoured throughout the land of Norway.

The Mark on the Donkey

Once, says an old story from Italy, the world was a happy place. God had made a garden and in it everything was at peace. The tiger and the elephant were friends and the roar of the lion hunting for the kill was never heard. Even the camel looked happy and the donkey roamed among them with a voice like a golden bell.

Then the Creator made man and sent him walking into the garden. At first, the animals were astonished, but they were polite and said nothing. Except the donkey. He looked at the man with no tail walking on two legs and, throwing back his head, he sent peals of laughter echoing through the garden. Suddenly his golden voice changed to a horrible braying sound. The garden was stilled as the Creator spoke, 'Thou shalt make that sound until the end of the world and for ever carry man as his beast of burden.' And so it has always been.

Hundreds of years went by and the donkey continued to make his horrible braying sound and to carry the weight of man and his belongings. This was his punishment for laughing at the work of God and he patiently bore his burden. Because he was so patient, God forgave the donkey and gave him a mark to show His forgiveness. It happened like this.

One day, two men came into an Eastern village and untied the colt of a donkey, which was tethered to a door in an open street, and led him to their Master. The poor little donkey was terribly frightened, for no one had ridden him before. Then suddenly, he heard a gentle voice and kind hands stroked his neck and ears. Cloaks were put on his back and, gently, the Rider drove him towards Jerusalem. As the donkey entered the city, he heard a great noise. Voices were shouting, 'Hosanna! Hosanna to the Son of David!' and branches of palm were strewn at his feet. But he was not frightened now that he had those calm Hands guiding him.

And then, as Jesus slipped from his back, a new mark was seen on the donkey's grey coat. It was in the shape of a cross—a brown cross down his back and across his shoulders.

This mark of the cross every donkey has borne to this day—a sign that he has been forgiven and for one glorious hour took his part in a day that shall never be forgotten.

The Young Man in the White Sheet

After the last supper together, Jesus and His disciples left quietly to go to the Mount of Olives. But not before Judas had slipped away into the night to go and betray his Master.

It was very late when Jesus and His disciples set out and no one was about in the dark, deserted streets. They thought they were unseen when they left the house, but someone had seen them go. A young man followed. He had a linen sheet wrapped about him so, surely, he had been in bed when Jesus and His friends passed by. Perhaps he had jumped up quickly and pulled the sheet around him, so that he would waste no time in dressing in case he lost Jesus and His disciples in the darkness. If he had jumped out of bed in a hurry, then he must have been sleeping in the house where the last supper was eaten. Perhaps he had heard footsteps coming down the outside stairway and, as he was young, he felt he must see the end of this night's mysterious happenings.

Through the dark and eerie streets the young man followed, keeping his distance in case he was discovered and sent back. His heart was beating wildly, for he felt that something terrible was going to happen that night but, although he was frightened, he crept on and on right through the city gates and out into the countryside. Down the steep sides of a ravine, across a valley and up the green slope beyond, he followed Jesus and His friends until they came to the Garden of Gethsemane.

Here, Jesus went on alone to pray. The disciples waited at a distance, and the young man crouched down still further away. His eyes were peering into the darkness and his ears were straining to catch every sound when, suddenly, behind him out of the night came Judas leading a band of rough soldiers armed with swords. The young man shivered for he knew they had come to harm Jesus and His

205

friends, but it was too late to warn them. The soldiers rushed forward and seized Jesus, and then the young man heard the sound of running feet. It was the disciples as they fled into the darkness, leaving Jesus to face the danger alone.

The young man's heart swelled within him. He would not forsake the Leader. Gathering his sheet about him, he crept forward. Then, one of the soldiers saw a gleam of white and seized hold of him. The young man's courage quickly faded; with a wrench, he tore himself away and ran, leaving the sheet gripped in the hand of the soldier.

Only St. Mark tells us about this young man. Perhaps it was himself and it was his own story. Years afterwards, people used to call Mark 'stump fingered' and perhaps he got that name because the soldier who seized hold of him slashed with his sword and cut off the top of one of Mark's fingers as they clutched the sheet. No wonder Mark let go and ran away. But, although like all the disciples, he forsook Jesus at that time we shall always be grateful to him because he wrote down for us the Life of our Lord.

Pandora's Box

Long, long ago, when the world was a very happy place and no one had even heard about sickness or disease, there lived a beautiful maiden named Pandora. Before her marriage to a King, she was given a lovely ivory box as a wedding present, and around the box was a clasp of gold.

With a messenger, Pandora set off for the country of the king but, as they were crossing a stream, she dropped the box into the water.

'I should leave it where it is,' said the messenger, 'that box will bring nothing but trouble.'

'Trouble!' said a voice from the box.

'What was that?' said the frightened Pandora.

'It is only Echo,' replied the messenger. 'Echo is allowed to repeat only the ends of the words she hears and, you see, she is warning you against the box.'

But Pandora wanted her box back again and the messenger, shrugging his shoulders, pulled it out of the water. On they went until they came to the King's palace and, here, the messenger left Pandora.

'Never open the box,' he said before he left. But, once inside the palace, Pandora became very curious. For a long time she sat and looked at the lovely ivory box with the golden clasp and, as she looked, she became more and more inquisitive.

'A little peep would do no harm,' she whispered to herself, and slowly and carefully she lifted the lid. Then, with a cry, she sprang back and tried to close the box again, but it was too late. Before she had time to slam the lid down, a great swarm of little winged creatures flew out of the box pinching and stinging. One stung her on the cheek and, at once, she had a headache, something she had never had before. People everywhere began to fight and quarrel in the streets and children began to cry and squabble among themselves. All the evils in the world had come out of Pandora's box and try as she would she could not stop them, for they were Troubles and flew everywhere giving people sickness and selfishness, unhappiness and disease.

'Silly woman,' they said to Pandora, 'why did you open the box?' But it was too late, for evil had spread over all the earth.

At last, Pandora managed to close the lid of her box and then she heard a tiny voice saying, 'Let me out! I am Hope the good fairy!'

At first, Pandora would not listen but then she opened the box again. From the bottom of the box there flew a shining bird and as it flew around Pandora's head it sang.

'I am Hope and as I stole into the box so shall I steal into the hearts of people everywhere.' With that, Hope flew about undoing all the evils that the Troubles had begun.

Today, countries join together to fight sickness and disease with medicines and the skill of doctors, for they too bring Hope to the peoples of the world.

The King of the Birds

Once upon a time, when all the birds of the air were gathered together, they began to quarrel among themselves as to who was to be king of them all.

'Which bird shall it be?' said the robin, 'how shall we choose our King?'

'Let us choose the one that flies the furthest,' said the pigeon.

'No!' said the sparrow, 'let us choose the one who flies the swiftest.'

'I think he should be the most beautiful bird,' said the peacock.

'The bird who sings the best should be king,' replied the nightingale.

'I say that the strongest should be king,' said the eagle.

The owl sat a little way off in the old oak tree and said nothing. But he looked so wise that all the birds said together, 'Let us ask the owl to choose for us.'

Off they flew to the old oak tree to ask the owl, who blinked and looked wiser than before.

'The bird that flies the highest should be king,' hooted the owl, and they all agreed.

But the wren, who is very small, said to herself, 'They think the owl is wise, but I am wiser than he, and I know which bird can fly the highest.'

Then all the birds began to stretch their wings and, when the signal was given, they all flew into the air to see who could fly above them all. Up and up they went, big and small together, and at last they found that the smallest birds could get no higher. One by one they sank down and down to the earth, until only the lark and the eagle were left. Soon, the lark could get no higher and the eagle soared up into the blue sky, the highest of them all.

'The eagle is our king!' cried all the birds on the ground and they waited to greet him as he swooped down to the earth. But then it was seen that perched on the top of the eagle's head was the tiny wren. She had chosen the biggest bird of all to carry her and had risen the highest of all.

'I am the king,' said the wren as she hopped down, 'for I went higher than the eagle.'

The other birds did not know what to do, so again they went to the old oak tree to ask the owl. The owl blinked two or three times and looked to the north, the south, the east, and the west.

'The wren did not fly at all,' hooted the owl sadly, 'for she was carried on the eagle's head. The eagle is king, for he not only flew the highest of all but he carried the wren as well'.

'Good, good!' cried all the birds as they hopped up and down.
'The owl is the wisest bird that flies and we will do what he says. The eagle is king over us all.'

The little wren crept out of sight. She thought that she was wiser than the owl, but now she really knows what is best for her. For, today, she always flies close to the earth and never tries to be anything than little Jenny Wren, as God has made her.

The Legend of the Dipper

There was once a little girl who lived with her mother in a little house in the woods. They were quite, quite alone for no one lived near them, but they were always very happy—as happy as the day was long. But one day the mother became very ill and it seemed that she would never be strong and well again.

'I must have a drink of clear, cold water,' she cried one night, as she lay in bed. 'I'm sure that that would make me well again.'

The night was very dark and there was no neighbour to ask for water, so the little girl took her tin dipper, which is like a big ladle or spoon, and she started out alone to the spring to bring her mother a drink. It was a long way through the woods and, being such a tiny girl, she was tired when she got to the spring. But she filled her dipper with water and started for home.

Sometimes she spilt the water because it was not easy to carry and sometimes the water spilled because she stumbled over the stones in the dark road. Suddenly she felt a warm touch on her hand. It was a little dog who had been following her for he, too, was very thirsty and had licked her hand with his hot tongue.

There was, by now, only a little water in the dipper but the girl poured a few drips into her hand and the thirsty dog lapped them up. Then a wonderful thing happened—although the little girl could not see it in the dark. The tin dipper was changed to silver with more water in it than before.

The little girl hurried on for she knew that her mother was waiting but she had not gone very far when she met a stranger on the road. He begged for a drink of cold water. Now the little girl knew that she must be kind to those in need, so she held up the water for him to drink. Then the silver dipper changed to gold, full to the brim with sparkling water, but still the little girl did not see it in the dark.

On the little girl went along the dark road for she was getting very tired and it was a long way to the cottage. By now she was very thirsty. The little dog had had a drink of water and so had the stranger. Perhaps it was her turn now. But no, her mother would need all that was left and she hurried on, carefully holding the dipper so that not a drop would be spilt. At last, she came to the cottage and hurried to her mother's bedside. And then came the greatest wonder of all. As soon as her mother drank of the water, she became quite well again and the gold dipper, as it touched her lips, was changed to one of diamonds—all shining and glittering with beautiful gems.

And then the diamond dipper left her fingers to shine up in the night sky, over the cottage and the woods and every town and city. There it shines every night to tell all children how once a little girl was brave and unselfish and kind.

The Kind Raindrop

There was once a farmer who had a large field of corn. He looked after it and weeded it with the greatest care, for he wanted to sell the corn and buy good things for his family with the money. But after he had worked very hard he saw the corn wither and droop, for no rain fell, and he began to fear that he would have no crop and no food for his family. He felt very sad, and every morning he went out to the field and looked at the thirsty stalks and then up at the sky and wished for the rain to fall.

One day, as the farmer stood looking up at the sky, two little raindrops saw him, and one said to the other, 'Look at that farmer. He looks so unhappy that I feel sorry for him. He took such a lot of trouble with his field of corn, and now it is drying up and withering away. I wish I could help him.'

'Yes,' said the other, 'but you are only one little raindrop. What can you do—except to drop on his nose?'

'Well,' said the first, 'I know that I am only one small raindrop and cannot do much to help but, perhaps, I can make the farmer a little more cheerful and I am going to do my best. If I can't do anything more, I will fall on the field and show that I want to help him. Here I go!'

The first raindrop had no sooner started on his way to the field than the second one said, 'Well, if you really must go then I think I'll come with you. Here I come!' And down went the raindrops one after the other. One came—splash!—on to the farmer's nose, and one fell on a thirsty stalk of corn.

'Dear me,' said the farmer, 'what's that? A raindrop? Where did it come from? I do believe we shall have a shower.'

By this time, a great many raindrops had come together to see what all the fuss was about. When they saw the two kind little raindrops going down to make the farmer happy and to water his field of corn, one said, 'If those two are going on such a kind errand, then I'll go too!' And down he came.

'And I,' said another.

'Don't forget me!' said a third.

'I'm coming too,' said a fourth.

And so said they all, as one after another they tumbled out of the sky, until a whole April shower was falling on to the field of corn below.

Then the corn grew and ripened and the farmer was very happy because the crop was saved and he had food for his family. And it all happened because one little raindrop tried to do what it could, even though it was so small.

Young John Mark

In a house in Jerusalem there once lived a boy named John Mark. His mother, Mary, was a Christian and often the disciples of Jesus came to their house. Sometimes, Mark helped his mother to shelter them—even Peter who had escaped from the prison of the wicked King Herod.

One day, his uncle Barnabas, brought to the house a little man with sharp eyes and a quick tongue.

'This,' said his uncle, 'is Saul of Tarsus, whose Greek name is Paul.'

It was, of course, the great St. Paul, and he and Barnabas were planning another long journey into unknown country to preach the words of Jesus. As they left the house, Barnabas said to Paul, 'Let us take young John Mark with us,' and Paul agreed.

So the three of them set off for Cyprus and walked right across the island, with Paul and Barnabas preaching in the villages as they went. Mark was very busy finding places to stay the night and getting their food, and he was very happy. When they got to the other side of the island, Paul wanted to cross the sea to another country, so Mark went to the harbour and arranged for a boat to take them across the water.

They crossed the sea and prepared to go on, but then John Mark became afraid. Paul, he heard, was planning to go over a great range of mountains by a lonely road where robbers and bandits lay waiting to attack travellers who went that way.

'This is madness,' said young John Mark, 'I'm not going.' And when he found a ship that was about to sail for home, he left quickly. His courage had failed him.

Four years later, Paul and Barnabas arrived back in Jerusalem after their great adventure and John Mark hurried to meet them and to say how sorry he was that he had been afraid. His uncle Barnabas forgave him and, when they set off on another journey, he wanted John Mark to join them again. But Paul said, 'No! John Mark left us when we had need of him. He let us down and he is not to come.'

So strongly did Barnabas feel that Mark should have another chance that, sadly, he left Paul and went off on another journey, taking John Mark with him.

Mark had a second chance and this time he did not fail. Years later, when Paul was a prisoner in Rome, chained to the soldiers who were guarding him, it was Mark who stayed by his side. Paul forgave young John Mark and, to show how much he trusted him, he sent Mark to visit the churches in the very country where, once, he had been afraid to go.

Mark also served Peter when he came to Rome and, as this was a dangerous time for Christians, he wrote down all that Peter could remember about his days with Jesus. Whenever Peter began, 'I remember when our Lord was talking . . .' Mark hastily wrote it down

211

and from all these stories we have, now, the Gospel according to St. Mark in the New Testament.

A Husband for Miss Mole

In the month of May, the babies of the mole are born in their little nursery under the ground. Once upon a time, a family of moles lived underneath a great tree and they were very happy in their tiny home. Now, Mr. and Mrs. Mole were very proud of their new daughter, Miss Mole, and when she grew up they wanted her to marry someone very great and important—not just another mole who lived under the ground.

Everyone agreed that the Great Blue Sky was the grandest and most splendid thing they knew, so off went Mr. Mole to ask the Sky to marry his daughter. To his surprise, the Sky replied, 'No, I'm not the greatest in the world. The Sun is my ruler and it is he who gives me my bright colours. You'd better go and see him.' So off went Mr. Mole to see the Sun.

'Alas! I am not the master,' said the Sun. 'The Cloud can cover me and stop my bright rays from burning. Go and see him.'

Away went Mr. Mole to catch the Cloud that was floating by. As the Cloud came nearer, pouring down the rain upon the earth, Mr. Mole went up to him. 'Excuse me,' he quavered, as the raindrops soaked his nice fur coat, 'are you the greatest thing in the world?'

'Can't stop to talk to you,' said the Cloud. 'My master the Wind is blowing me away. Ask him . . . ask him,' and the Cloud disappeared into the distance, leaving but a whisper behind him.

Then up roared the Wind, blowing all before him. 'Am I the greatest thing?' he puffed, 'why, bless you, no! There's a great rock on Earth that hasn't moved or blinked for me in a thousand years and I've been blowing at him hard enough.'

So, rather tired by this time, Mr. Mole came down to Earth and going up to the Great Rock, asked him if he was the greatest thing in the world.

'Indeed, I am great!' said the Rock. 'The Sun may burn but he never bothers me. The Wind may blow but I am unmoved. The Rain may pour in torrents but it only slides off my back. No, the Sun, the Wind, and the Rain are no trouble to me.'

The Great Rock thought for a moment, then he said, 'But there lives under my feet a wretched Mole. He digs and digs and digs and one of these days he'll topple me right over. You'd better go and see him.'

So, at last, Mr. Mole found the right husband for his daughter and never again did he travel the world looking for something that was next door to him.

The Pig Brother

There was once a child who was very untidy. He left his books on the floor, and his muddy shoes on the table; he put his fingers in the jampot and spilled ink on to his clean shirt; there was no end to his untidiness. One day, the Tidy Angel, came into his room. 'This will never do!' said the Angel. 'This is very bad. You must go and stay with your brother while I set things right here.'

'I have no brother!' said the child.

'Yes you have,' said the Angel. 'You may not know him, but he will know you. Go out into the garden and watch for him, and he will soon come.'

'I don't know what you mean,' said the child: but he went out into the garden and waited. Presently along came a squirrel.

'Are you my brother?' asked the child.

The squirrel looked him over carefully. 'I should hope not!' he said. 'My fur is neat and smooth, my nest is clean and tidy, and my young ones are properly brought up. Why do you insult me by asking such a question?'

He whisked off, and the child waited. Presently a wren came hopping by.

'Are you my brother?' asked the child.

'No, indeed!' said the wren. 'What impertinence. There is no tidier person than I in the whole garden. Not a feather of mine is out of place and my eggs are the wonder of all for smoothness and beauty. Brother, indeed!'

He hopped off, ruffling his feathers, and the child waited.

By and by a large tommy cat came along.

'Are you my brother?' asked the child.

'Go and look at yourself in the mirror,' said the cat proudly, 'and you will have the answer. I have been washing myself in the sun all morning, while it is clear that you haven't washed for a long time. There is no one like you in my family, I am glad to say,' and he walked on waving his tail.

Presently a pig came trotting along. The child did not wish to ask the pig if he were his brother, but the pig did not wait to be asked, 'Hallo, brother,' he grunted.

'I am not your brother,' said the child.

'Oh, yes, you are,' said the pig. 'I confess I am not proud of you, but there is no mistaking the members of our family. Come along

213

and have a good roll in the barnyard! There is some lovely black mud there.'

'I don't like to roll in the mud!' said the child.

'Tell that to the hens,' said Pig Brother. 'Look at your hands and your shoes, and your clothes! Come along, I say! You may have some of the pig-wash for supper, if there is more than I want.'

'I don't want pig-wash,' said the child, and he began to cry.

Just then the Tidy Angel came out. 'I have set everything to rights,' she said, 'and so it must stay. Now, will you go with the Pig Brother, or will you come back with me, and be a tidy child?'

'With you, with you!' cried the child, and he clung to the Angel's dress.

The Pig Brother grunted. 'Small loss,' he said. 'There will be all the more pig-wash for me to eat.' And he trotted off to the barnyard.

The Miller, the Son, and the Donkey

One fine day, in the early morning, a miller and his son were taking a donkey to the market so that they could sell it and get a good price. The sun was shining and the sky was blue as the miller, his son and the donkey with a clip-clop-clip-clop, made their way towards the town. They had not gone very far along the road when they were met by some girls.

'You are silly,' they said, 'walking to market. Why don't you ride on the donkey?'

The miller, hearing this, told his son to get on the donkey and on they went along the road with a clip-clop-clip-clop, towards the town. After a while they met two old men and one old man said to the other. 'Why is that young fellow riding on the donkey, while his poor old father has to walk? Isn't that just like these selfish youngsters nowadays!'

Rather red in the face, the miller's son hurriedly jumped off the donkey and helped his father to mount and on they went along the road, with a clip-clop-clip-clop, towards the town.

Soon they came to a farm where there were some women working in the fields. As they went by, the women looked over the hedge and shouted angrily to the miller. 'You cruel man! There you are riding comfortably on the donkey while your poor little son has to walk. You ought to be ashamed of yourself.'

The miller, who was really a very kind-hearted man, at once told his son to get up behind him and the two on the donkey jogged slowly into the town with a clip-clop-clip-clop.

As they drew near to the houses, they were stopped by a shepherd who said to the miller. 'Excuse me, but does that donkey belong to you?'

'Indeed, it does,' said the miller, 'why do you ask?'

'Because that is not the way to treat a donkey,' replied the shepherd. 'Two of you on its back is too much for the poor animal. Why, you two are far better able to carry the donkey than he to carry you.'

At once the miller and his son jumped down and tying the donkey to a pole, began to carry it between them across the narrow bridge that led to the market place. All the people came out of the shops and houses to watch the strange sight of a donkey being carried on a pole and they laughed so loudly that the donkey took fright and began to struggle. In trying to hold him, the miller and his son slipped on the edge of the bridge and, with a splash, they fell into the river. They suffered no more than a wetting, but the miller was a much wiser man and decided to think for himself in the future.

The Prayer from Iona

Once, long long ago on the island of Iona, there lived a company of monks. The leader was a good man called Columba, and from the rocky shore of Iona they could see the other islands across the waves. One day they all went down to the seashore and, putting food and water into a little boat called a coracle, they said goodbye to one of the monks named Cormac who was going to a distant island to tell others about God.

'Our brother Cormac is going on a long and dangerous journey,' said Columba. 'Let us pray to God for his safety.' So they knelt down on the seashore and prayed that God would be with him always. Then Cormac got into his little boat and they watched him sail away until he was lost to sight.

That night they prayed for him, and the next day Columba said 'Pray for him, too, while you are working.'

So when the monks were copying books and writing words from the Bible they remembered to say a prayer for Cormac. When those who were in the fields came to the end of planting a row of seeds, they remembered to pray for Cormac. When the monk who was in the kitchen lifted the pots from the fire he, too, remembered to pray for Cormac's safety.

The days and nights went by and, because they were so busy with their work, the monks began to forget to pray for Cormac. They had so many things to do that soon they forgot the extra prayers completely. Then came the storms of winter. The wind howled across the island and they were all very glad that they were snug and safe indoors and not one of them gave a thought to Cormac out on the wild sea.

Suddenly, above the howling of the wind, they heard the sound of the great bell which called the monks to church.

'What can it mean?' they said. 'It is not the time for prayers now'.

But they all wrapped their cloaks about them and battled through the wind to the wooden chapel. There they found Columba ringing the great bell.

'My brothers,' he said, 'have you thought what this stormy weather will mean to those who are out on the rough sea? Have you remembered our brother Cormac? Just now he may be in great danger and we promised to pray for him.'

The monks were ashamed that they had forgotten to pray and, there and then, they knelt down to pray for Cormac's safety.

Several mornings later one of the monks saw a speck far out on the white-capped waves. As it came nearer, he saw that it was a boat and he called the others down to the shore. It was Cormac's boat and soon he landed safely on the shingle.

'Four days ago,' he said, 'there was a terrible storm. The boat was almost sinking and I was afraid. Then I remembered that you had promised to pray for me and, suddenly, I felt strong and brave again and fought on against the waves. Your prayers made all the difference.'

The monks looked at one another. How glad they were that Columba had reminded them to pray again.

The Abbey Church at West Minster

Many years ago, two streams flowed into the River Thames from the northern side just before London. Between the two streams was a small island of gravel and sand called the Isle of Thorns or Thorney Island. On this island a band of monks began to build an abbey which they dedicated to St. Peter.

One night, a poor Lambeth fisherman called Edric was fishing in the river. For many days he had caught nothing and now he hoped to make a good haul of fish so that he could sell it at Billingsgate Market and get money for his wife and children. But his luck was out, for although he tried again and again, nothing could he catch. Disappointed, he decided to go home and, gripping the oars, he rowed for the shore. Suddenly, he heard a voice calling him and on the river bank he saw a man standing there.

'Take me to the Isle of Thorns,' called the man, 'and I will give you a rich reward.'

216

By now it was very late and getting dark, but the fisherman was a kindly man and helping the stranger into the boat he rowed him to the island.

'Wait here,' said the stranger, as the boat grounded on the shingle, and stepping on to the shore he disappeared into the empty abbey which stood on the island.

In the gathering darkness Edric the fisherman waited, with only the sound of the tide as it bumped his boat against the stony shore. Suddenly, the half built abbey church blazed with light and the fisherman saw angels descending from above. He heard the sound of music soaring from the empty church and there was the scent of sweet-smelling incense around him.

When the stranger returned, the fisherman dropped to his knees in fright.

'Fear not,' said the man, 'for I promised you a rich reward. Cast your net once more into the water and you will make a catch.'

At once the fisherman did as he was told and immediately the net was full to overflowing with a great haul of salmon.

'Take one of them,' said the stranger, 'to Millitus, Bishop of London, and tell him that the fisherman of Galilee has blessed his church and all that shall worship therein.'

Many years later, on that same island, Edward the Confessor, who was the last of the Saxon Kings, rebuilt a great abbey in the shape of a cross. Because it lay to the west of London they called it West Minster and as Westminster Abbey it has become one of the most famous cathedrals in the world.

In the Beginning

In the beginning, God made the world. He made the sun to rule the day and the moon and stars for the night. Now there came a time when the Earth rose from the waters and presently tender grass began to grow and trees appeared on the hills. Fish swam in the waters and birds flew to and fro among the forests and animals could be seen in the mountains. And, last of all, God made Man in the garden of the world.

As the years went by, God saw that many of the men on His earth were wicked and had evil thoughts in their hearts. 'I will destroy them all,' said the Lord, 'for I am sorry I made them.'

But there was one good man named Noah and God said to him, 'I am going to destroy everything on earth with a flood. Make an ark of wood and take two of every living thing into the ark with your family. Take food enough for all and you will be saved.'

217

So Noah did as God told him and, when all were safely inside the ark, the rains began to fall. For forty days and forty nights it rained and the face of the earth was covered with water. Everything was destroyed and only Noah and those with him in the ark were saved. Then God sent a wind to pass over the earth and the waters began to go down and once more the land was dry. Noah went out, and his sons and his wife and his son's wives too. Every animal and living thing went out of the ark that day and Noah thanked God for their safety.

Sons were born to the sons of Noah after the flood. And they became the fathers of the nations of the earth. Everyone in those days had the same language and speech.

'Let us build a city here on the plain,' they said. 'And in the city let us build a tower whose top shall reach to the heaven.' So they made bricks and mortar and they built their city and in the city they started their tower that went up towards heaven.

And God saw the city and the tower and He said, 'With one people and one language this is what they begin to do. There is nothing they will not try.'

So God made them speak different languages and they could not understand each other any more. As they did not understand each other, they could not work together and they gave up building the tower and scattered over all the world.

Many, many years later, the Son of God came upon earth to teach men to live together and to work together in peace and goodwill. And when Jesus left His people, He said to His followers, 'Go forth and make all nations my disciples . . . and be assured, I am with you always, to the end of time.'

The Fair Children of Angle Land

One day, a man called Gregory was walking through the market place in Rome. He was a good man and leader, or Abbot, of a monastery nearby. As he walked through the market he passed the fruit stalls piled with purple grapes and golden oranges. He passed the stalls with meat and bread and the merchants shouting their prices and he came to a corner of the market where they were selling children as slaves. He noticed their blue eyes and golden hair because they were different from the sunburnt children of his own country.

'Where do these fair haired children come from?' he asked.

'They are heathens from Britain,' was the reply, 'and they are called Angles.'

'Angles!' said Father Gregory, 'they look more like angels than Angles. Have they never heard about God and his love for us all?'

'No,' said the man, 'no one has ever been to their island to tell them.'

From that moment, Gregory made up his mind to go to Angle-land, or England as it is now called, and take the message of Jesus. As soon as he could, Gregory set off but on the journey he was called back to Rome and later became the Pope. But he never forgot his promise and he sent Augustine, from his own monastery, to go in his place to the land of the Angles.

It was a dangerous journey, but at last Augustine and his band of forty good men landed on the shores of England. It was a lovely spring morning, on that day more than a thousand years ago, and the sun gleamed on the silver cross they carried and on a picture of Jesus painted on wood.

The king wanted to hear their message, but he was afraid that Augustine and his men were magicians. In those days they thought that no magic could be done in the open air, so the king met Augustine out in the fields.

The king listened as Augustine told why he had come and the story of Jesus and the One True God and he treated them kindly and let Augustine and his men live near his palace in the city of Canterbury.

By Christmas Day, over ten thousand people had been baptised and Augustine built a church at Canterbury and became head of all the Christians in England, the first Archbishop of Canterbury.

And when the fair-haired boys and girls were christened in church, they were given Christian names, because the Message of Jesus had come to the land of the Angles.

The First Whitsuntide

Peter and the other disciples were together in the Upper Room of a house in Jerusalem. Below them, they could hear the noise of the crowd as they surged along the streets. It was quiet in that room and they remembered what had happened at the last feast when that same crowd were shouting, 'Crucify Him! Crucify Him!' as they watched Jesus being led before the Roman Governor.

Peter was thinking of the words of Jesus when He had given him His last command, 'You will receive power when the Holy Spirit comes upon you; and you will bear witness for me in Jerusalem and all over Judea and Samaria, and away to the ends of the earth.'

Suddenly, in that quiet Upper Room, there came a sound of a

mighty wind rushing through the house and it seemed to fill that little room where they were sitting. Then they all saw a glowing light which appeared to break up into little tongues of flame and to hover over the head of each one of them.

The effect on them was tremendous. They were filled with great power. Peter wanted to tell everyone about Jesus. He was no longer afraid of the crowd in the streets below and he leaped to his feet and went hurrying across the flat roof top to the low wall which was at the edge. Peter looked down. He saw the street filled with an excited crowd of people. Perhaps they had heard the sound of the rushing wind. But, here they were, and Peter saw in a flash that this was a wonderful chance to tell people about Jesus.

As Peter raised his hand for silence a hush fell on the crowd and raising his voice Peter spoke out boldly. He knew that it might be the same crowd who only a few weeks before had shouted for the death of Jesus—but he had no fear. As he spoke, the crowd were amazed for they could understand every word that he said.

'Is he not a Galilean?' they said. 'Then how can he speak in our languages—the Medes, the Arabians, the Elamites. How does he speak in our own tongue?'

On that day, that first Whitsun, three thousand of them were baptised and became followers of Jesus. In this wonderful way the Christian Church was born and day by day has grown stronger.

Every year, since that day nearly two thousand years ago, the Christian Church has kept three great Festivals. They are Christmas, when Jesus was born in Bethlehem; Easter, when He was crucified and rose from the dead; and Whitsuntide, when He sent His Holy Spirit upon those who follow Him and long to spread His message to all people.

Brothers of the Holy Trinity

Once upon a time, in the country of France, there lived two friends called Felix and Jean. They did not live in a house in a street, but in a hut in a great forest among the tall trees. No one lived near them; they were all alone except for the wild creatures and the birds. They had come there to be quiet and alone with God and they put their trust in God so that they never felt lonely or unhappy.

One day Jean said to Felix, 'It is not enough that we should live alone in peace and quiet. Over the sea in Africa there are Christians who once were as free as we are, but now they are slaves—prisoners of savage people who keep them in chains. They cannot go free unless a large sum of money is paid. Let us go together and pay for their freedom.' So the two set off out of the forest.

220

First they went to the Bishop who gave them his blessing.

'You shall wear,' he said, 'a white cloak with a red and blue cross on your shoulder and you shall call yourselves the Brothers of the Holy Trinity.'

It was not long before others wanted to join Jean and Felix on their adventure and when, altogether, they had collected enough money to go on their journey and to pay for the freedom of the poor Christian slaves in Africa, they set off on their travels.

First they travelled across the land of France until they came to the Mediterranean Sea. Then they went on board a large wooden sailing boat and sailed across the blue sea to Africa where the Christian slaves were kept as prisoners.

Jean went boldly to the savage people who kept the Christians as prisoners and said, 'We have brought you gold to buy the freedom of the Christians. Will you set them free?' And he gave the savage people the bags of money.

The iron chains were taken from the slaves and joyfully they all made their way back to the coast where the wooden sailing boat was waiting. As the sails were set they filled with the breeze and their boat sailed out to sea.

But as they left the harbour they saw that a strange ship was following. Quickly it came alongside, filled with the savage people, who leaped on board their boat and threw the steering helm into the sea. Then their swords flashed in the sun as they tore great holes in the sails and, leaping back on to their own ship, they left the Trinity Brothers and the Christian slaves to drift helplessly out to sea—perhaps to drown.

But Jean did not lose heart. 'Trust in God and He will guide us,' said Jean, 'and for sails we will use our cloaks.' So they took off their white cloaks with red and blue crosses and hung them up for sails. Then, as they knelt in prayer, there came a strong breeze. As their cloaks filled, the boat moved forward and they sailed happily over the waves until they all came to land in safety.

The Forgotten Treasure

If you search in the woods during the month of June, you may find the forget-me-not and this is how it got its name.

There was once a shepherd who found a tiny blue flower so beautiful that he had never seen one like it before. He tied it to his shepherd's staff and went on towards home. Suddenly, a small figure sprang out from behind the trees.

221

'You lucky man,' he said, 'what a treasure you have to be sure. Take that flower with you and touch that rock with it over there. The rock will open up and, inside, you will find gold and silver and diamonds. Take what you want. But, remember, don't forget the best.' And, with that, the little figure disappeared.

The shepherd stood there for a moment, wondering what he should do. Then, taking the blue flower from his staff, he laid it gently against the rock. At once, there was a rumbling noise and slowly the rock opened to show a doorway with steps that led inside. Fearfully, the shepherd entered and going slowly down the steps one by one, he gazed about him. As his eyes got used to the dark, he saw heaps of gold and silver and diamonds sparkling in the gloom and winking at him from the floor of the cave.

Quickly, the shepherd laid down the tiny blue flower and, seizing the bag that was on his shoulder, he began to scoop up as much treasure as he could. He piled the wealth into his bag and as his hands scooped up the treasure he heard a tiny voice saying, 'Don't forget the best! Don't forget the best!'

But the shepherd could think of nothing but the gold, the silver and the diamonds, and when he had gathered as much as he could carry, he hurried away leaving the little blue flower behind. As he came into the open air, the rock closed behind him with a crash.

As fast as his legs could carry him, the shepherd hurried home to show the treasure to his family. 'Look what I have found!' he said, as he threw his bag upon the table.

Quickly, his family gathered around him but, when the bag was opened, there was nothing inside—nothing but dust and ashes. Then the shepherd remembered. He had forgotten the little blue flower that he had found for the first time.

As fast as his legs could carry him, the shepherd hurried back running all the way. But when he got there, the rock was closed and there was no way in.

Then, faintly, he heard these words, 'Forget-me-not! Forget-me-not!'

Anxiously grasping for the riches, the shepherd had left the best lying forgotten.

Brittany Gold

Across the sea, in the land of Brittany, there are many fine fields of waving corn but once, long long ago, there was none. This is how corn came to be grown in the land of Brittany.

There was once a good man named St. Leonore and he lived with a company of friends called monks. They lived in a monastery and around them were beautiful meadows with sparkling streams and fields of golden corn. They were very happy in this garden of England and they were never hungry because they had the flour from the corn to make into bread.

But, one day, St. Leonore heard that the people across the sea, in the land of Brittany, were hungry and starving. They knew nothing of God who cares for us all, and they fought and robbed and killed each other for the little food that there was.

'Let us go to them,' said Leonore, 'and tell them the good news of Jesus, so that they will help one another and live together in peace and goodwill.'

So they went down to the seashore and set off in a wooden boat for the land of Brittany. They took with them the things they would need in the new land; tools to build houses, cloth to make clothes, and seed to grow corn so that they would never be hungry. But, on the way across the sea, there was a great storm and their boat was wrecked. St. Leonore and his friends came safely to land but the tools, the cloth and the seed went down to the bottom of the sea.

With difficulty, they built themselves a hut to live in and St. Leonore put up a wooden cross around which he taught the people about Jesus. Sometimes the birds, especially the robin, came to sit on it because the monks were so friendly. But, the people were starving and, one day, when there was even less food than usual, Leonore said, 'We must help these poor people to grow corn so that they will have bread to eat in winter.'

And with his friends he cleared a piece of gorseland round the cross, turning up the rich black earth with pointed sticks and making a wall of stones around it.

'But where is the seed?' asked the monks, knowing that no one could go back across the stormy sea to fetch it from England.

'God will send us that,' said Leonore and, day after day, they prayed and waited. Then, one morning, in the season for sowing, they saw a robin flying over the field. It settled on the wooden cross and as they came nearer, it dropped from its beak a whole ear of corn.

With great care, they took the golden grains from the ear of wheat and planted them carefully one by one in the little field they had made ready. Next season, they reaped a tiny harvest of wheat stalks, each with its head of grain. This was all planted again—and, in a few years, corn-fields were everywhere with food for all in summer and winter. God had provided for those who trusted in Him.

The Children's Victory

Once, long ago, a city was surrounded by a great army. For many days, the army had been attacking this city and the people inside were weary with fighting as they defended the gates and the walls. They had been without food for a long time and, now, they were starving and knew that soon they must open the gates and surrender.

One morning a man named Wolff, who had been defending the city walls, was going slowly home very tired after wearing his armour throughout the night. He knew that all this fighting was useless for, next day, they would be forced to surrender through lack of food.

At that moment, he passed by a large orchard full of cherry trees that were covered with ripe cherries, and a thought came into his mind. If they were hungry and thirsty so, too, must be the army fighting to get into the city. Arrows and spears and stones had been no good—perhaps the kindness of a gift would work a miracle.

Quickly, he put his plan into action for he knew he must not waste a moment while lives were being lost. Going from house to house and street to street he went through the city, gathering together as many children as he could. He told them to wear white as a sign of peace and, at last, he had three hundred children gathered together. Into their arms he put the large bunches of fruit from the cherry orchard and, as he threw open the city gates, the children walked out on their strange journey.

When the leader of the army saw the gates open, he thought that the city had surrendered. Then he saw three hundred white-robed children coming towards him.

'What is this trick?' he shouted and he raised his arm to give the order to shoot a flight of arrows into the children walking towards them.

Then, something wonderful happened. As the children came nearer the soldiers could see that they were laden with fruit as a gift and a shout of welcome came from them. They put down their weapons and greeted the children with open arms, taking and eating the fresh fruit which they had not seen for a long time. The leader of the army knew that he was conquered. Not by strength of arms, but by the power of kindness and pity.

When the children returned to the city, the army went away from the city walls and left them all in peace never to return again.

For many years afterwards, when that day came round, it was kept as a holiday and called 'The Feast of Cherries'. On that day, children went through the city in white robes carrying bunches of cherries to remember the victory that was won by the children.

It was in the middle of June, in the year 1215, that king John of England was made to sign the Great Charter or Magna Carta, which gave rights and freedom to the people for all time.

King John had a hasty temper and was always afraid that someone might rise up against him and seize his throne. When he heard that the Abbot of Canterbury had a fine house with many servants, he became jealous and afraid that the Abbot had become too powerful. So he sent for the Abbot of Canterbury and said to him, 'Unless you can answer me three questions, you will be thrown into prison!'

'What are those three questions, my lord?' said the Abbot who was, of course, very frightened.

'First,' said the King, 'how much am I worth? Second—how long would it take me to ride round the world? And third—what am I thinking?'

Now the Abbot could find no answer to these three questions and he was in great distress. He begged for three weeks in which to answer them and this request was granted. As the days went by, he could find no one to answer these questions—even the wisest men in the kingdom. Towards the end of the third week, the Abbot was riding home sadly when he met an old shepherd.

'Why are you so sad?' asked the shepherd and the Abbot told him.

'I will answer the questions for you,' said the shepherd, 'if you will let me dress in your rich robes and pretend that I am the Abbot of Canterbury.'

To this the Abbot agreed and the shepherd went before the King, disguised in the robes. The King greeted him and asked the first question: 'How much am I worth?'

'The Bible tells us that Jesus Himself was sold for thirty pence,' was the reply, 'so you cannot be worth more than twenty nine.'

The King could not say this was wrong, so he asked the second question: 'How long would it take me to ride round the world?'

'If you rise with the sun and ride with the sun until it rises the next morning—then you will have ridden round the world.'

Again the King was outwitted but with the third question, he was sure that there was no answer: 'Tell me what I am thinking now?'

'Your Majesty,' was the reply, 'you are thinking that I am the Abbot of Canterbury. But I am not—I'm only a humble shepherd.'

And with that, he took off the rich robes and stood revealed as the shepherd that he was.

The King laughed so much that he forgave the trick that the wise old shepherd had played on him, and the Abbot of Canterbury was left in peace until the end of his days.

The Saint of Holywell Hill

Once, long ago, when the Romans were in Britain, there lived a man called Alban. He was a rich man and he lived in a fine house not far from London. Now, Alban knew nothing of Jesus and he worshipped heathen gods like most of the people in those days. At this time, the Roman soldiers were killing the Christians and, one summer afternoon, an old man came to the house of Alban to beg for shelter.

'Lord,' said the old man, 'Roman soldiers seek my life. Will you give me shelter, for I know that you are a kind man?'

'What have you done,' said Alban, 'that the soldiers seek your life?'

'I have done no evil,' replied the old man, 'but I am a Christian priest and follow the teaching of Jesus. For this, they are going to kill me.'

'Come in!' said Alban, 'and I will give you shelter.'

For many days, the priest hid in Alban's house and Alban brought him food and water and took care of him. He saw how calm and brave the priest was, although he was in great danger, and Alban began to wonder whether he, too, could become a Christian.

'Tell me of the God you worship!' Alban asked, and the priest told him of God the Father of us all and the message of Jesus, and Alban became a Christian. Then, one day, there came a loud knocking at the door. The soldiers had heard where the priest was hiding and had come to take him away.

'Farewell, my son,' said the priest to Alban. 'My time has come and I am not afraid. I thank you and I go—to die.'

'Not so!' replied Alban. 'Give me your robe! Take my cloak and wrap it about you. Here is gold for your journey. Go out by the secret way and may God be with you!'

Quickly, they changed clothes and the priest, dressed as Alban, escaped by a secret way. A few moments later, the soldiers burst into the room and seeing a man in a long robe and deep hood of a Christian priest, they dragged him before the governor.

When they pulled the hood from Alban's head and the governor saw that it was not the Christian priest, he was very angry at being tricked. 'I ask your name!' he shouted.

'Does it matter?' replied Alban, 'I am just—a Christian.'

'Because you have hidden a Christian priest,' said the governor, 'and now stand in his place, you must suffer his punishment.'

226

Then Alban was led out across the river and up a hillside, gay with summer flowers, to the place of execution.

'This is a holy man,' said the soldier who walked beside him. 'I cannot kill him!' and he threw down his sword.

'For that,' said the captain of the guard, 'you will, also, be punished.'

On the flower covered hilltop, Alban and the Roman soldier were put to death. A spring of water appeared nearby and, to this day, the hill is called Holywell Hill and Alban's town is called St. Alban's.

Why Summer Days are Longer

Long, long ago, at the beginning of time, the Sun used to race across the sky very quickly. Everyone grumbled because it made the day so short. There was little time to go hunting or fishing and there was not enough daylight to do all the work they had to do.

A fisherman, called Mani, thought that he would teach the Sun a lesson. 'Why!' he said, 'should the Sun race across the sky so quickly? Perhaps, if I can slow him down we shall have more hours of sunshine in which to fish and sail our boats!'

So, being a fisherman, he plaited long ropes to make a net or snare. Then, one summer morning before the dawn, he got into his canoe and sailed far out across the sea to the very edge of earth, where the Sun rose from beneath the ocean. Bobbing on the waves in his little boat, Mani cast his net across the sea and waited.

Soon, the Sun began to rise and before he knew what was happening he was fairly caught in Mani's net. Then Mani pulled the ropes tight and the Sun had to stand still.

'O Sun,' said Mani, shielding his eyes from the glare, 'why do you race across the sky from the east to the west? You give us no time to do our work!'

'Please let me out of the net!' replied the Sun. 'I have a long journey in front of me.'

But Mani held on tight and refused to let go.

The sun shone very brightly. 'I shall be late,' he said, 'and the seas must be warmed and the corn ripened in many lands.'

But Mani held on to the net more tightly, even though some of the ropes were burning.

'I have an idea,' said the Sun, 'and if you will let me out of the net, I promise to tell you.'

Carefully, Mani loosened the net but he wisely refused to take off all the ropes in case the Sun did not keep his word.

227

The Sun rose higher in the heavens. 'Perhaps,' he said, 'if I stand still and let the earth travel round me, you will get your longer days —but only in the summertime.'

To this Mani agreed and, letting go of the net, he paddled his canoe back to the shore as the Sun beamed down upon him.

And that is how it has been to this day. The ropes of Mani, the fisherman, may still be seen hanging from the Sun at dawn and at night, but we call them the Sun's rays. The days are longer in summertime, but the longest day of the year was when Mani cast his net and made the Sun stand still.

Peter and John at the Beautiful Gate

One day Peter and his friend John were going to the Temple Church, for it was three o'clock in the afternoon and the time for prayers. Many other people were going too, so Peter and John went through the crowds until they reached the lovely gate that led into the Temple courtyard. It was called the Beautiful Gate.

As they reached the Beautiful Gate they heard someone calling out. It was a beggar who was lame and could not walk and he was asking for money so that he could buy bread to eat. Every day he was carried there by his friends and for forty years he had sat in the same place.

The cripple, seeing Peter and John, lifted his hands to beg for a coin and Peter said to him, 'Look at us.' The lame man looked up quickly, hoping to get a very big coin from this kind man.

But Peter said, 'I have no silver or gold; but what I have I give you; in the name of Jesus Christ of Nazareth—walk.' Then Peter grasped the beggar by the right hand and pulled him up. At once the lame man's feet and ankles became strong. He sprang up and stood on his feet. 'Look! I can walk!' he shouted, and leaping and running he went before them through the Beautiful Gate.

Hearing the noise, a big crowd gathered to see this wonderful sight. Peter spoke to them all about Jesus the Son of God and many who were listening became Christians. But, as Peter was talking, soldiers pushed their way through the crowd and both Peter and John were taken away to prison.

'What are we going to do with these men who are friends of Jesus?' asked the rulers and chief priests. 'Everyone knows that they have cured a man who has been lame for forty years.' So, after warning Peter and John not to talk about Jesus, they let them go.

But, by now, a great number of people had become followers and many believed that if only the shadow of Peter fell on a sick man he would be cured. The chief priests became so angry that they put Peter and John into prison again.

That night the prison doors swung open and an angel of the Lord brought them out and said, 'Go to the temple and speak to the people about this new life and all it means.' So Peter and John went to the Temple and began teaching again.

The next morning, when the soldiers went to the prison, they found all the doors were locked and no one was inside. The chief priests were very puzzled until a man came to them and said, 'Look! the men you put in prison are out in the Temple teaching the people.'

Again, Peter and John were brought before the chief priests who were so angry that they wanted to kill them. But one of their number spoke out and warned the priests that if this was the work of God, then nothing could stop Peter and John. So they let them go free and every day they went on telling the good news of Jesus.

A Little Drop of Water

One fine day, long long ago, a dewdrop (which is a tiny drop of water) was clinging to the petal of a lovely, red rose.

'How nice it is to be here,' thought the dewdrop. 'Here am I, clinging to the petal of this lovely rose and enjoying the scent and colour of the flowers. The sun is warm, and all around me is the countryside with its green grass and tall trees and singing birds. Yes! I could live here for ever.'

But, just then, there came the faint whisper of a breeze and the dewdrop began to roll down the petal of the rose. In vain, he tried to cling on but he only rolled faster and faster down the slippery petal until, with a plop, he fell to the ground.

'Oh, dear,' said the dewdrop, 'and I was so comfortable up there on the rose petal. But, never mind, the green grass is very soft and I can listen to the bees and look up at the blue sky.'

As he lay there, he was soon joined by another drop of water, and another, and another, until they were all trickling through the grass and heather and rolling down the hill until they came to a tiny brook, singing among the stones.

'This is fun,' said the dewdrop as he tumbled among the stones, sparkling and flashing in the sunlight. 'I wonder where we are going?'

Just then the brook flowed into a stream, dropping over little waterfalls as it wandered through the woods and the dewdrop was carried on to a swiftly flowing river. Sometimes he was in a little quiet pool by the river bank, with the fish darting to and fro, and sometimes he was carried to the middle of the river, helping to carry the boats that were floating by.

'I never knew the world was like this,' thought the dewdrop as he was carried on by the broad river, 'I wonder what will happen next?'

Then he heard a strange loud noise that he had never heard before and there was a salty taste in his mouth. Rolling and tumbling and dipping and twisting, he found himself in the sea with the waves breaking on the seashore and the tides sweeping the golden sands.

'This is the end of me,' said the dewdrop as down and down and down he went to the bottom of the ocean. As he floated along among the seaweed, crabs and starfish he felt very tiny among the millions and millions of drops of water all around him.

'How sad I am to leave the lovely countryside,' he said to himself. 'All is finished for me now,' and feeling very sorry for himself he crept into a dark shell and, laying down on a tiny grain of sand, he went to sleep. A long, long time went by and, one day, the shell was found by a diver. Inside was the dewdrop, but now he was changed to a lovely pearl, all glistening and shimmering in the sunlight. Today, he stands in the middle of an emperor's crown, still giving pleasure to all who see him, and he knows that God's world is full of wonderful surprises.

The Creeper that turns Crimson

In the beginning when God first made the world, He made the sky a lovely blue colour with clouds of silver and white. Then God made the plants of the Earth with stalks and leaves of green and, when these were finished, He painted the flowers last of all.

As He passed by, the flowers reached out to Him and were painted in lovely colours—blue for the cornflower and yellow for the daffodil, white and purple for the lilac and a deep red colour for the rose. But there was one little plant growing at the foot of an old, bare rock. She was too small and too shy to stretch out her tiny flower to be painted as God passed by and her tiny blossom was left in green.

The poor little plant felt very sad when she saw the lovely colours of the other flowers and she wondered what she could do.

Soon, the sun came out and shone on all the brightly coloured flowers but the old, bare rock, where the little plant was growing, began to scorch and crack in the heat of the sunshine.

'This heat is terrible!' he groaned and the little plant felt sorry for him.

'I will cover him with my green leaves,' she thought and she began to grow and to climb higher and higher until she had covered the old, bare rock from the rays of the sun with her tiny leaves.

230

One day, when the autumn had come, God sent down an angel to see all the flowers He had made. The angel went across the fields and the meadows and along the rivers and the streams and saw many beautiful growing things. At last, he came to the old, bare rock which he knew so well. But there was no rock to be seen. A beautiful green plant with tiny leaves had covered it over and the angel saw the kindness that had caused this to happen.

'This plant has no colour except green,' he said, 'but it is the most beautiful of them all.'

The little green plant heard and blushed. She blushed a beautiful crimson colour—a colour more beautiful than all the flowers.

And every year, when autumn comes, the little plant remembers the praise of the angel, and blushes again when she thinks of it. But, now, we call her the Virginia Creeper.

The First Butterflies

When God first made the world He covered the earth with a cloak of green; the fields He made gay with flowers and the forests bright with many coloured birds. And in the blue waters of the sea, God put the sea creatures and fish of every kind.

And God said, 'My children will love the fields, the forests and the seas and the gentle beauty of the earth around them. But how will I get them to love the mountains? They look so dark and cold and yet they have a beauty of their own. How can I get the people on earth to go to them and so learn to love them?'

For many days God thought about the mountains. At last, He made many little shiny stones. Some were red, some blue, some green, some yellow and some were clear and bright with all the lovely colours of the rainbow. And God took these precious stones, the rubies, the sapphires, the emeralds, and the diamonds and He hid them among the seams and cracks in the mountains. 'Now, men will come to seek them out,' He said, 'and they will learn to love the mountains and the high places on earth.'

But when the precious stones were placed and God looked again upon their beauty, He said, 'I will not hide all of you away under the rocks and in dark places. Some of you will be sparkling in the sunshine, so that children who cannot go to the mountains will see your colours.'

At that moment, the South Wind came by and as he went he sang softly of the fields clothed in green, of forests flecked with sunlight and of birds and nests in leafy trees. He sang of long summer days and the music of the waves upon the shore—of starlight and moon-light. The song of the South Wind was a thanksgiving for all the beauties of the earth.

And God was pleased with the song of the South Wind and He said, 'Take these things to carry away with you to your summer home, so that all the children of the world will love them.' At these words, all the brightly-coloured stones that God held in His hand stirred with life and lifted themselves on many–coloured wings. They fluttered away in the sunshine and the South Wind sang to them as they went.

So it was that the first butterflies flew into the world and in their wings are all the colours of the shining stones that God did not wish to hide away in the mountains.

When Jesus was Thirsty

An old legend says that once, long ago, when Jesus was abroad in the world, He wandered across the grasslands of a country called Hungary.

It was a hot day and the sun blazed down on the open fields and, because He had walked a long way, Jesus was very thirsty. Suddenly, in the distance, He saw a well and he turned towards it with the hope of getting a drink of water.

As He came nearer, Jesus saw a man lying down by the well in the shade of a leafy tree. He was a herdsman taking his rest after the midday meal and nearby was his herd of cattle. The cattle were standing quietly together in the noonday sun and all was at peace as they munched at the sweet grass or dozed in the heat.

'Kind friend,' said Jesus to the man, 'I have come from afar in the heat of the sun. Will you give me a drink of water to quench my great thirst?'

The man hardly lifted his head at the words of Jesus and, although he had plenty of water in the jug by his side, he pointed with bad grace to the well and said, 'The well is there and the water is at the bottom. Drop the bucket down for yourself if you want a drink.'

Jesus said nothing, but helping Himself to water from the well He quenched His thirst and went on His way across the grasslands. As He walked, He talked to people He met on the way; the workers in the fields, the farm hands, and the tillers of the soil and again Jesus became thirsty because of the great heat. He saw another well in the distance and turned towards it. Near the well, Jesus saw a shepherd who was having great trouble with his flock of sheep. The sheep were running this way and that way, plagued by swarms of flies, and the poor shepherd did not know what to do to keep them safely together.

'Kind friend,' said Jesus to the shepherd, 'I have come from afar in the heat of the sun. Will you give me a drink of water to quench my great thirst?'

Although he was so troubled with his sheep, the shepherd at once took pity on the lonely stranger. Telling Jesus to sit down, he went to the well and filling his own jug with cold, fresh water he turned to offer it to Jesus. As he did so, he was surprised to see his sheep coming quietly together to stand in a flock, and not one of them was missing.

And from that day, when the summer sun beats down upon the fields, the sheep will flock quietly together when the shepherd takes his midday rest. But the cattle, with tossing heads and swishing tails, are restless and plagued with flies. The herdsman cannot rest because once, one of their number would not take pity on a thirsty Stranger.

The Angel of the Trees

Out in the woods there grew a little pine tree and its leaves were long, slender, green needles. But the pine tree did not like its needle-sharp leaves. 'I wish that I had different leaves,' it thought. 'Better even than the oak, or the beech, or the willow. If I could have my wish, I would have leaves of shining gold.'

That night, the Angel of the Trees walked through the woods and, when the little pine tree awoke the next morning, all its leaves had turned to shining gold.

'How beautiful I am!' thought the pine tree, 'with my gold leaves sparkling in the sun. The oak, the beech and the willow look so dull beside me.'

Foolish little pine tree! That night, a man stole into the woods with a bag and passing the oak, the beech, and the willow, he went to the pine tree and picked off all the gold leaves and took them home.

'Oh, what shall I do?' said the pine tree, next morning. 'I will not wish for gold leaves again. Perhaps leaves of glass would sparkle in the sun just as well. I wish that I could have glass leaves.'

That night, the Angel of the Trees walked through the woods again and, in the morning, the pine tree sparkled with leaves of crystal glass. But, in the afternoon, black clouds hid the sun, the thunder rolled and the rain poured down. A strong wind shook the little pine tree and, soon, there were no glass leaves to sparkle when

233

the sun came out. Nothing but broken glass lay at the foot of the little pine tree.

'I will not wish for better leaves than my neighbours,' said the tree. 'If I had nice green leaves like the oak, the beech, and the willow, I would be happy again.'

Then the pine tree went to sleep and once more the Angel of the Trees walked through the woods. When morning came, the pine tree looked just like all the other trees for it had fine, large, green leaves. But the big leaves looked so juicy and tempting that an old goat came along and ate up every one for his dinner.

'Alas!' cried the little pine tree. 'A man took my leaves of gold, the wind broke my leaves of glass and, now, an old goat has eaten all my green leaves. If only I had long, green needles back again!'

All this time, the Angel of the Trees had been listening to everything that the little tree said. The next day, when the birds flew to the pine tree they were glad to see that it was covered again with its long, green needles. They were happy to build their nests there again, safe and warm for the winter when it comes.

'Gold leaves, glass leaves, and large green leaves were very fine,' said the birds, 'but there's nothing better for a little pine tree than its own long green needles.'

Jesus by the Seaside

One day, Jesus and His disciples went by boat to a lonely beach on the Sea of Galilee. They went there to rest, but the crowd followed them along the seashore and, when the boat grounded on the pebbly beach, hundreds of people were waiting. Jesus felt sorry for them, so He and the disciples climbed a hillside and the crowd gathered around them. Then Jesus taught them many things and healed the sick.

By this time, it was getting late and the sun was setting beyond the western hills. The disciples became anxious and said to Jesus, 'It is very late and this is a lonely place. Shall we send them away to buy food?'

Jesus replied, 'There is no need for them to go; give them something to eat yourselves.'

'But twenty pounds would not buy enough for them all,' replied Philip.

And then Andrew spoke up: 'There is a boy here who has five barley loaves and two small fishes. But what is that among so many?'

Quietly Jesus said, 'Make the people sit down.' And the five thousand that were there sat down on the green grass of the hillside.

Jesus then gave thanks to God and, taking the loaves, He broke them into pieces and gave them to the disciples to give to the five thousand. He did the same with the two fishes and they all had as much as they could eat and the scraps that were left over filled twelve great baskets.

When the meal was over, Jesus told His disciples to go down to the boat and go on before Him to the other side of the Sea of Galilee. Jesus stayed behind to persuade the great crowd of people to go home. By this time, it was quite dark and Jesus, instead of going to sleep, went alone up the hillside to pray.

Hour after hour passed by and the disciples were far out to sea. By now a strong wind was blowing, throwing up huge waves and, although they were rowing as hard as they could, they were making no progress. There was no one to help them for Jesus was alone on the land. Suddenly, in the half-light of the morning, they saw Him coming towards them walking on the waves. They thought it was a ghost and cried out in fear.

But, at once Jesus called to them. 'It is I; do not be afraid.'

Then Peter called out, 'Lord, if it is you, tell me to come to you over the water!'

'Come,' said Jesus, and Peter stepped down from the boat and started to walk over the sea towards Him. But when Peter saw the furious waves and the blackness beneath him, he became afraid. He began to sink and cried out, 'Lord, save me!'

Jesus at once reached out His hand and caught hold of Peter. 'Why did you hesitate?' He said, 'How little faith you have!'

They then climbed into the boat and, as they did so, the wind dropped and the waves calmed. All those that were on board were amazed and they came to worship Him, saying, 'Truly you are the Son of God.'

The Golden Apples

Long, long ago, there lived in the land of Greece a beautiful girl named Atalanta. She was a princess and when she was born her father, the King, was so disappointed that he had no son to rule after him, that he left Atalanta on a high mountain to the mercy of the cold winds and the wild animals.

However, Atalanta was saved by some hunters who took care of her and trained her to run swiftly so that she could catch deer and the antelope that they were hunting.

When, at last, Atalanta returned to her father's palace, she could run so fast that there was not a boy or girl in the land who could out-run her in the foot race.

Now the time came for Atalanta to marry but her father found it difficult to decide who was the best youth for her to wed.

'As my daughter can run faster than anyone in the land,' he declared, 'any youth who can out-run her in a race shall have her hand in marriage. But should he lose that race, then he shall also lose his life.'

Hearing this, many of the young men who had come forward for the challenge, hastily withdrew from the race. Others who were foolish enough to take part were quickly out-run and they lost their lives.

Many came forward and many were beaten but, at last a clever youth named Milamon succeeded in beating Atalanta. Milamon brought with him a gift of three golden apples which he carried hidden beneath his tunic. These apples were made of shining gold and no one could resist their beauty.

Soon the race began and, as they sped along the course, Atalanta as usual easily passed the young man. But as she sped onward, a golden apple rolled past her feet. For a moment she hesitated and then turned aside to pick up the precious fruit. At once, Milamon raced past her but soon Atalanta had regained the lead. Then the youth dropped the second apple and, again, Atalanta stopped to pick it up. Quickly she made up the lost distance but she had to run her hardest to do so. Atalanta had all but won the race when Milamon tossed the third golden apple in her path and, as the third golden apple came rolling to her feet, Atalanta stopped to pick it up. But, this time, although she ran faster than ever before, it was too late to overtake the young man and Milamon was first past the winning post.

So Atalanta lost the race and, true to the promise, married the young man who had added brains to his feet.

The Legend of St. Christopher

Once there lived a man called Offero, as tall and strong as a giant. He was so strong that he could pull up the forest trees by the roots or crush a man with one hand, but he never hurt so much as a tiny sparrow, for he was good and kind.

When he was young, Offero took his armour and sword and set out to serve the strongest king in all the world. For a while he fought in the army of a great king but he discovered that this king was frightened of the Evil One. So Offero left him and went on to find the Evil One of whom everyone was afraid. In the depths of a black forest he found this Evil King and served him for many years.

But, one day, when Offero was out riding with him, he saw the King turn away from a wooden cross set up on a hill.

'What!' said Offero, 'are you the bravest king on earth and fear a piece of wood?'

'It is not the cross I fear,' said the Evil One, 'but Him who once hung there.'

So Offero left the service of the Evil King who was afraid and journeyed on to find the King who was stronger.

At last, he came to the banks of a mighty river, wide and fast flowing. There he met a hermit and Offero asked him where the King of the Cross could be found.

'Everywhere,' said the hermit, 'and if you would serve Him you must pray.'

'That I cannot do,' said Offero. 'But I have great strength. Bid me serve Him in another way.'

So the hermit took Offero to the wide and angry river and told him to live there and carry across all who wanted to get to the other side. Offero was surprised at so humble a task, but he built himself a hut and tore up a pine tree for a staff. Then day after day and night after night he carried across the angry flood all those who wanted to cross.

Then, one night, there was a terrible storm and Offero heard a tiny voice crying, 'Offero! Offero! Will you carry me across?'

At first, Offero could not believe that anyone would want to cross on such a night but, taking his lantern and staff, he went out into the storm and found a little Child waiting for him on the bank of the river. Lifting the Child into his strong arms he waded into the water, thinking what a light burden he carried. But, as he went, the Child grew heavier and heavier, so that it took all his strength to go on. The waves came up to his shoulders and it seemed that he would never get to the other side but, at last, he struggled to the bank and set down his Burden safely.

'Child, who art thou?' he said. 'The whole world upon my shoulders could not have been heavier than you have been.'

Suddenly the storm ceased and a light shone about the little Child.

'You have indeed borne the world on your shoulders,' said the Child, 'for you have carried Him who bears the sorrows of the world. And because you have been so kind to the weak and have carried Christ on your shoulders, you shall be called Christopher, the Christ-bearer.'

Then the Child vanished and Christopher knew that he had found the strongest King at last and he served Him joyfully all his days.

237

ACKNOWLEDGMENTS

STORIES: *The Burning of the Rice Harvest* (adapted from *Gleanings in Buddhafields*, Kegan Paul). *Hans the Shepherd Boy* (from *Stories for Character Training*, Harrap). *The Little Girl who would not work; The First Christmas Tree; The Angel of the Flowers; The Kind Raindrop* (adapted from *For the Children's Hour*, Geo. Philip & Son). *The Monastery on the Island* (*Talking to Children*, R. Clifford Smith, Lutterworth). *The Journey of Mary and Joseph; The Prayer from Iona* (Religious Education Press). *The Lonely Shepherd* (adapted from *Christ Legends*, Selma Lagerlof). *The White Feather of Friendship, Two Stories* (*500 Tales to Tell Again*, H. L. Gee, Epworth). *Martin the Cobbler* (adapted from Tolstoi's *Where Love is, God is*). *The Silver Candlesticks* (from *Les Miserables*, Victor Hugo). *The Pig Brother* (from the *Golden Windows*, Laura E. Richards, Allenson Ltd.).

POEMS: *Autumn Leaves; Kindness to Animals; What was it Like?; The Christmas Tree; Come away to Bethlehem; White World; Mother's Hands; Birds' Nests; June Wind; Yellow; The Sea Shell* (Evans Bros.). *Out in the fields with God; Christmastide; The Shepherds Slept; God is so Good* (*Poems of Praise*, Collins). *God's Providence* (Nancy Boyd Turner). *Every Day* (Mary Osborn, SPCK). *The Fairy Flute* (Rose Fyleman, Reprinted by permission of *Punch*). *The Three Kings* (*The Cowley Carol Book*). *The Friendly Beasts* (Robert Davis, Schmitt, Hall & McCreary). *Four Things* (Henry Van Dyke, Chas. Scribners & Sons). *The Voice of God; James Stephens* (Macmillan & Co.). *Just for Jesus* (Lysbeth Boyd Borie, J. B. Lippincott Co.). *The Wind* (R. L. Stevenson). *Spring* (P. M. Bolger, A. H. Stockwell Ltd.). *The Stars* (Christina Rosetti). *The Country Faith* (Norman Gale). *The Song of the Trees* (*Child Songs*, The Pilgrim Press).

Every effort has been made to trace the source of copyright material and it is regretted if any acknowledgement has been unwittingly omitted.